TRANSPORTATION INFRASTRUCTURE -
ROADS, HIGHWAYS, BRIDGES, AIRPORTS AND MASS TRANSIT

SLOT-CONTROLLED AIRPORTS

CONGESTION, CAPACITY, AND COMPETITION ISSUES

TRANSPORTATION INFRASTRUCTURE - ROADS, HIGHWAYS, BRIDGES, AIRPORTS AND MASS TRANSIT

Additional books in this series can be found on Nova's website under the Series tab.

Additional E-books in this series can be found on Nova's website under the E-book tab.

TRANSPORTATION ISSUES, POLICIES AND R&D

Additional books in this series can be found on Nova's website under the Series tab.

Additional E-books in this series can be found on Nova's website under the E-book tab.

TRANSPORTATION INFRASTRUCTURE -
ROADS, HIGHWAYS, BRIDGES, AIRPORTS AND MASS TRANSIT

SLOT-CONTROLLED AIRPORTS

CONGESTION, CAPACITY, AND COMPETITION ISSUES

OWEN M. WHITAKER
EDITOR

nova publishers
New York

For permission to use material from this book please contact us:
Telephone 631-231-7269; Fax 631-231-8175
Web Site: http://www.novapublishers.com

Additional color graphics may be available in the e-book version of this book.

Library of Congress Cataloging-in-Publication Data

ISBN: 978-1-62948-350-4

Published by Nova Science Publishers, Inc. † New York

CONTENTS

PREFACE

This book reviews the effects of adding more beyond-perimeter flights from Reagan National; and how well slot control rules are working to reduce congestion, while maximizing capacity and encouraging competition. Also discussed are slot allocation and airline schedule data using a statistical model, and interviews with FAA officials and others.

Chapter 1 – To help manage airport congestion, airlines operating at four U.S. airports—Washington's Reagan National and the three major New York City area airports—must obtain operating authorizations called slots from FAA to take off or land. Airlines operating out of Reagan National also may not operate flights beyond a 1,250-mile perimeter without congressional approval. In addition to the 24 flights (12 round trips) previously approved, Congress recently authorized 16 more beyond-perimeter flights (8 round-trips) at Reagan National—flights that the airport authority fears will adversely affect Reagan National and the authority's ability to continue servicing its debt. Some airlines seeking to serve slot-controlled airports assert that slot control rules cause the airports to be underutilized or used inefficiently. GAO was asked to review (1) the effects of adding more beyond-perimeter flights from Reagan National and (2) how well slot control rules are working to reduce congestion, while maximizing capacity and encouraging competition. GAO analyzed slot allocation and airline schedule data, developed a statistical model, and interviewed FAA officials and others.

Chapter 2 – In 1999, GAO reported that Reagan National Airport could accommodate at least 36 more slots, which are authorizations from DOT for a takeoff or landing. In 2000 and 2003, two federal statutes, known as AIR-21 and Vision 100, permitted DOT to award 44 new slots to airlines, 24 of which could be used for flights to cities more than 1,250 miles, which was the statutorily mandated limit for non stop flights from Reagan National. The DOT awards went to airlines serving six cities (Denver, Las Vegas, Los Angeles, Phoenix, Salt Lake City, and Seattle). For this year's reauthorization of the FAA, GAO was asked for an update on the capacity of Reagan National to accommodate additional slots and the effect of relaxing the perimeter rule. GAO updated its 1999 study to answer these key questions: (1) To what extent can Reagan National accommodate additional flights? (2) Since AIR-21 and Vision 100, what changes have occurred in market share and fares for flights operating between the six beyond-perimeter cities and the three Washington, D.C., area airports? In commenting on this report, DOT and the airports authority generally agree with our findings but with one exception, the airports authority disagrees with DOT's estimate of slots because it disputes their methodological assumptions. We believe the department's methodology for estimating airport capacity is appropriate.

In: Slot-Controlled Airports
Editor: Owen M. Whitaker

ISBN: 978-1-62948-350-4

Chapter 1

SLOT-CONTROLLED AIRPORTS: FAA'S RULES COULD BE IMPROVED TO ENHANCE COMPETITION AND USE OF AVAILABLE CAPACITY*

United States Government Accountability Office

WHY GAO DID THIS STUDY

To help manage airport congestion, airlines operating at four U.S. airports—Washington's Reagan National and the three major New York City area airports—must obtain operating authorizations called slots from FAA to take off or land. Airlines operating out of Reagan National also may not operate flights beyond a 1,250-mile perimeter without congressional approval. In addition to the 24 flights (12 round trips) previously approved, Congress recently authorized 16 more beyond-perimeter flights (8 round-trips) at Reagan National—flights that the airport authority fears will adversely affect Reagan National and the authority's ability to continue servicing its debt. Some airlines seeking to serve slot-controlled airports assert that slot control rules cause the airports to be underutilized or used inefficiently. GAO was asked to review (1) the effects of adding more beyond-perimeter flights from

* This is an edited, reformatted and augmented version of United States Government Accountability Office, Publication No. GAO-12-902, dated September 2012.

Reagan National and (2) how well slot control rules are working to reduce congestion, while maximizing capacity and encouraging competition. GAO analyzed slot allocation and airline schedule data, developed a statistical model, and interviewed FAA officials and others.

WHAT GAO RECOMMENDS

Among other things, GAO recommends that FAA improve its administration of the slot control rules, including applying the utilization requirement to individual slots. Department of Transportation (DOT) and FAA provided technical comments, which GAO incorporated as appropriate, and agreed to consider the recommendations.

WHAT GAO FOUND

The 16 new beyond-perimeter flights that were authorized in 2012 for Reagan National Airport are likely to have a limited effect on the airports in the Washington, D.C., area. Reagan National has sufficient runway capacity to accommodate the new beyond-perimeter flights and, with some improvements to baggage handling and security screening facilities, will have sufficient terminal capacity. Reagan National is routinely operating below 67 hourly takeoffs and landings ("slots")—the maximum number authorized in any one hour—mostly because general aviation or other unscheduled aircraft operations decreased substantially after new security restrictions were imposed following the September 11, 2001, terrorist attacks. GAO's analysis found that the new beyond-perimeter flights could add a maximum of about 5 percent of 2011 passenger levels at Reagan National, and if all of that increase came from passengers moving from Dulles International or Baltimore-Washington International Thurgood Marshall, these airports could experience a maximum decline of 4.1 percent of 2011 passenger levels. As a result, because Reagan National and Dulles generally do not share what are largely fixed costs, passengers shifting from Dulles to the new beyond-perimeter flights at Reagan National would, in the worst-case scenario, increase average airline costs to use Dulles by about 4 percent. Similarly, the new beyond-perimeter flights are not likely to affect the Washington Metropolitan Airports Authority's (MWAA) ability to service its $5.2 billion debt for the two airports. Finally, because half of the new beyond-perimeter flights were awarded to low cost airlines, thereby increasing competition, these new flights could have a positive effect on airfares on routes where new flights were added.

Slot control rules help the Federal Aviation Administration (FAA) manage congestion at these four airports by limiting the number of takeoffs and landings that airlines may make per hour. The rules, however, in effect, allow some existing airport capacity to go unused, and this capacity is therefore unavailable to other airlines because airlines are not required to schedule a flight for each of their slots, but instead are only required to use their slots 80 percent of the time. Moreover, FAA's recordkeeping and its process for reviewing airlines' self-reported slot utilization data do not provide sufficient assurance that FAA can identify instances when airlines do not meet the 80 percent utilization requirement or determine how much capacity is going unused. In addition, FAA's allowing airlines to apply the requirement collectively to their pool of slots, rather than individual slots, further contributes to slots going unused and provides an advantage to airlines with large slot holdings. In addition to some existing capacity going unused, flights at the slot-controlled airports, even when operated, tend to be scheduled in such a way that available capacity is used more inefficiently than at like-sized airports that are not slot-controlled, thereby limiting passenger growth and access by new-entrant airlines that could offer new service or lower fares. For example, GAO found that flights operated at slot-controlled airports tend to be scheduled with smaller aircraft. Using statistical analyses, GAO found that scheduled passenger flights at slot-controlled airports are 75 percent more likely to be scheduled by airlines using an aircraft with fewer than 100 seats than flights at other like-sized airports that are not slot-controlled. Slot-controlled airports also tend to have certain routes that are flown at higher daily rates and aircraft that are less full.

ABBREVIATIONS

AIR-21	Wendell H. Ford Aviation Investment and Reform Act for the 21st Century
BWI	Baltimore Washington International Thurgood Marshall Airport
BTS	Bureau of Transportation Statistics
DOJ	Department of Justice
DOT	Department of Transportation

IATA	International Air Transport Association
FAA	Federal Aviation Administration
JFK	John F. Kennedy International Airport
MWAA	Metropolitan Washington Airports Authority
TSA	Transportation Security Administration

September 13, 2012
The Honorable John D. Rockefeller IV
Chairman

The Honorable Kay Bailey Hutchison
Ranking Member
Committee on Commerce, Science, and Transportation
United States Senate

For each takeoff or landing at Ronald Reagan Washington National Airport (Reagan National) and the three major New York City area airports—John F. Kennedy International (JFK), LaGuardia International (LaGuardia), and Newark Liberty International (Newark)—airlines must obtain an operating authorization, also known as a "slot,"[1] from the Federal Aviation Administration (FAA). Although more than 150 airports are slot-controlled throughout the world, including all major European airports, only these four airports are currently subject to slot controls in the United States. FAA started limiting the number of takeoffs and landings per hour at these airports more than 40 years ago because of congestion and delay. Reagan National is also subject to a federally-imposed 1,250-mile limit on the distance of nonstop flights to and from the airport, called the perimeter rule. However, on three occasions since 2000, federal statutes have been enacted requiring a total of 40 slot exemptions (20 round trips) to the perimeter rule, allowing nonstop flights to destinations more than 1,250 miles from the airport. This includes 16 more beyond-perimeter flights (8 round trips) required as part of the reauthorization of FAA in February 2012.[2] Although we reported in 1999 and 2007[3] that Reagan National could accommodate additional flights, the airport authority that operates Reagan National—the Metropolitan Washington Airports Authority (MWAA)—raised concerns about the airport's ability to accommodate these new beyond-perimeter flights as well as their effect on the other Washington, D.C., area airports and the ability of MWAA to continue servicing its $5.2 billion debt.

The New York City area airports are operating under temporary FAA orders, which constitute the current slot control rules that limit the number of takeoffs and landings for flights out of those airports. However, despite operating under slot control rules, these airports continue to be among the most delayed in the country, which in turn affects the efficiency of the nation's entire airspace system. Moreover, although the rules were designed to control congestion, while also maximizing the available airport capacity, some airlines seeking entry into these airports assert that the current rules do not adequately address inefficient uses of the constrained airspace and airport capacity, and that not enough of existing capacity is allocated to new entrants, restricting competition and access to the primary commercial airports in the region. They also assert that airlines currently operating out of these airports use their slots in ways that keep out competitors. To address these problems at the New York City area airports, FAA, which is responsible for managing congestion at airports, tried to implement rules in 2006 (that were revised in 2008) that, among other things, would have allowed FAA to auction some slots held by incumbents and, under one of the two options, keep the proceeds. In October 2009, before implementing any changes, FAA rescinded the final congestion management rules for the New York City area airports, in general, citing congressional and airline opposition to auctioning slots, among other things, and a federal court ruling.[4] In 2010, the Department of Transportation (DOT) began developing a "Slot Management and Transparency" rule for JFK, LaGuardia, and Newark to replace the temporary slot control rules under which they have been operating since 2006 for LaGuardia and since 2008 for JFK and Newark. These temporary rules have been extended twice, creating a level of uncertainty in the market about when the final rule will be issued and what it will contain.

In response to your request, we reviewed the potential effects of increasing the number of beyond-perimeter slot exemptions at Reagan National and whether slot control rules at the four U.S. slot-controlled airports are working to reduce congestion, while maximizing available capacity and encouraging competition.

To review the potential effects of increasing the number of beyond-perimeter slot exemptions at Reagan National, we

- compared the airport's airside capacity assessment with actual usage;
- reviewed terminal space needs;

- assessed the effects of the additional beyond-perimeter flights on security screening wait times, passenger traffic, capital financing, and aircraft noise; and
- interviewed officials from FAA, MWAA—which operates Reagan National and Dulles International Airport (Dulles)—and Baltimore-Washington International Thurgood Marshall Airport (BWI) as well as representatives from airlines and others.

To review whether slot controls at U.S. slot-controlled airports are working to reduce congestion while maximizing available capacity and encouraging competition, we compared and contrasted DOT data on flight delays, as well as airline schedule data on aircraft size, flight frequency, and other factors at slot-controlled airports with airports that are not slot-controlled. We also constructed a statistical model to assess whether flights at the slot-controlled airports are maximizing passenger throughput as compared with other large hub airports[5] that are not slot-controlled by examining aircraft size. We reviewed the reliability of the data used in our analyses and concluded that they were sufficiently reliable for our purposes. We also interviewed officials from DOT, FAA, the Department of Justice (DOJ), MWAA, and the Port Authority of New York and New Jersey, which operates the New York City area airports, and interviewed representatives from airlines and others. We conducted this performance audit from October 2011 to September 2012 in accordance with generally accepted government auditing standards. Those standards require that we plan and perform the audits to obtain sufficient, appropriate evidence to provide a reasonable basis for our findings and conclusions based on our audit objective. We believe that the evidence obtained provides a reasonable basis for our findings and conclusions based on our audit objectives. More details about our scope and methodology of our work are presented in appendix I.

BACKGROUND

The Washington, D.C., region and New York City area airports vary with regard to their size, proximity to downtown areas, and type of service provided. In the Washington, D.C., region, Reagan National is located in Arlington County, Virginia, near the nation's capital, while the two other major airports—Dulles and BWI—that are part of the Washington, D.C., area air passenger market are larger and located farther from city centers. While

Reagan National and BWI primarily provide domestic service, about one-fourth of enplanements at Dulles in 2011 were international. Reagan National and Dulles are owned by the federal government and are operated by MWAA under a 50-year lease that has been extended 30 years (1987-2067). Reagan National is subject to slot controls, but Dulles and BWI are not. In the New York City area, LaGuardia is located in Queens, near Manhattan, and primarily provides domestic air service, while JFK and Newark are larger airports that are located farther from Manhattan and provide more international service. Appendix II provides more detailed comparative information about the four slot-controlled airports, plus Dulles and BWI.

On-time flight performance at Reagan National is comparatively better than the other slot-controlled airports and cancellations and delays at the New York City area airports have been among the worst in the nation. According to on-time arrival performance data that airlines reported to the Bureau of Transportation Statistics (BTS) for 2011, among 29 major airports,[6] Reagan National ranked 22nd, JFK ranked 25th, LaGuardia ranked 27th, and Newark ranked 29th. Because, according to FAA, one-third of the approximately 50,000 aircraft that FAA guides through the national airspace system every day move through the New York area at some point during a typical day, delays in this region can have a disproportionate impact on airspace and airport delays experienced throughout the rest of the system. According to 2012 research conducted by the MITRE Corporation for FAA, one-third of the flights in the country are directly affected by delays in the New York City and Philadelphia areas. Furthermore, the rate of late arrivals and flight cancellations— another indicator of on-time performance—at the three New York City area airports was worse than the system-wide average during the last 10 years.[7] The rate of late arrivals and cancellations at Reagan National, however, was better than the system-wide average during 4 of the 10 years (see figure 1).

FAA previously relied on its statutory authority to manage airspace usage to implement slot controls through an FAA regulation called the High Density Rule, which capped the number of hourly arrivals and departures permitted at five designated "high density traffic airports"—LaGuardia, JFK, Newark, Washington National,[8] and Chicago O'Hare International— and, among other things, required airlines to obtain slots for these operations. The High Density Rule was implemented at Reagan National and the three New York City area airports in the late 1960s to reduce congestion and delay. Reagan National has remained slot-controlled under the High Density Rule since 1969, although there have been modifications to the operating limits and provisions of the rule throughout the years. On the other hand, rules at the New York City area airports have at times been relaxed or suspended as a result of statutory changes and FAA actions. For example, because of lessened concerns about congestion at Newark, FAA suspended slot controls at that airport from 1970 through 2008.

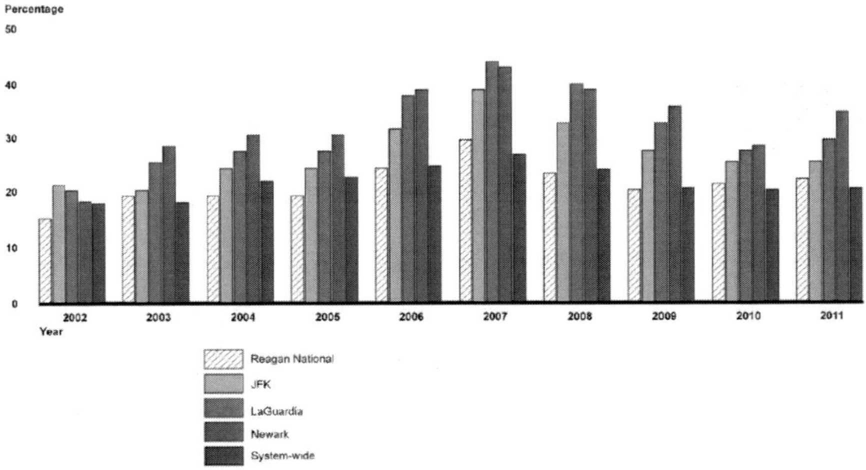

Source: GAO presentation of BTS data.

Note: In this figure, the percentage of delays and cancellations has been combined. The system-wide data include the four slot-controlled airports. Flights that arrived 15 minutes or more late compared with the scheduled time are counted as late arrivals. BTS data do not include international flights, which represented about half of the enplanements at JFK and about one-third of the enplanements at Newark in 2011.

Figure 1. Annual Percentage of Late Arrivals and Flight Cancellations at the Four Slot-Controlled Airports Compared with All Airports from 2002 through 2011.

In addition, in the 1990s, there was some perception that slot controls were a barrier to improved service, in part, because new airlines were unable to establish service at the slot-controlled airports. Subsequently, in 2000, the Wendell H. Ford Aviation Investment and Reform Act for the 21st Century required the High Density Rule to be phased out at JFK and LaGuardia by January 1, 2007. These 2000 statutory provisions also directed DOT, in the interim, to grant exemptions to the High Density Rule to allow for a limited number of flights operated by new entrant airlines and for flights serving small communities. As a result, airlines scheduled more flights at LaGuardia than the airport could handle without unreasonable delays. FAA subsequently issued temporary orders limiting scheduled operations at LaGuardia to 75 per hour in 2006 and at JFK and Newark to 81 per hour in 2008.[9] The limits at LaGuardia were based on the limits prior to the 2007 phase-out. In setting the limits on scheduled operations at JFK and Newark, FAA undertook an analysis that included modeling the estimated level of delay associated with various levels of operations. (As shown in fig. 1, from 2002 through 2011, the rate of late arrivals and flight cancellations at the slot-controlled airports and system-wide was greatest in 2007 when slot controls were not in effect at JFK and Newark.)

Before FAA adopted slot allocation and transfer rules, in 1985, airlines organized scheduling committees through which slots were allocated. In 1986, FAA, believing a secondary market in slots would address concerns by new entrant airlines and smaller carriers about access to and competition at High Density Rule-controlled airports, amended the rule to allow airlines to buy and sell slots. Under the temporary orders at the New York City area airports, imposed after the statutory expiration of the High Density Rule at JFK and LaGuardia, FAA allocated slots to airlines based on their current operating schedules at those airports in conjunction with voluntary airline schedule-reduction agreements or, in the case of LaGuardia, based on their current slot or slot exemptions holdings. To encourage competition at these airports under the High Density Rule, Congress also has periodically directed DOT to allocate slots exemptions to airlines operating new service at slot-controlled airports. Generally, once airlines have been allocated slots or slot exemptions, so long as they comply with the rules, they may keep them indefinitely[10] and consider them to be valuable assets.[11]

Although slot controls were designed to manage congestion by limiting the number of scheduled flight operations per hour at each of these airports, the rules also contain a provision designed to encourage use of airport capacity by requiring airlines to use their slots a minimum percentage of the time. Beginning in 1986, FAA's High Density Rule required airlines at specified airports to use their slots at least 65 percent of the time, but starting in 1992, they were required to use them at least 80 percent of the time. Although the 80 percent usage requirement is applicable to all four slot-controlled airports, other provisions of the rules differ between the airports, including

- the hours when airlines are required to have a slot to operate a flight,
- the time periods for which slots usage is measured and reported to FAA, and
- whether airlines can buy or sell slots (see table 1).

In general, at Reagan National and LaGuardia, slots are allocated for every day of the week and must be used at least 80 percent of time in a fixed, 2-month reporting period (e.g., January-February, March-April, etc.).[12] At JFK and Newark, slots are allocated for a specific day of the week and must be used at least 80 percent of the time for that day during a scheduling season.[13] Slots not used in accordance with the 80 percent rule are subject to withdrawal by FAA.

Additionally, because the slot rules at the New York City area airports are contained in temporary FAA orders and are not considered by FAA to be a long-term solution, slots may not be bought or sold at those airports.[14] Slots may be leased and traded, however, at any of the slot-controlled airports.

Table 1. Selected Slot Control Rule Provisions for the Four U.S. Slot-Controlled Airports

	Reagan National	LaGuardia	JFK	Newark
Minimum slot usage requirement	80 percent	80 percent	80 percent	80 percent
Hours that airport is slot-controlled	All hours	6:00 a.m. to 9:59 p.m., Eastern Time, Monday – Friday and 12:00 p.m. to 9:59 p.m., Eastern Time, Sunday	6:00 a.m. to 10:59 p.m., Eastern Time, daily	6:00 a.m. to 10:59 p.m., Eastern Time, daily
Usage measured for...	All days over 2-month reporting period	All days over 2-month reporting period	Each day of the week over a scheduling season[a]	Each day of the week over a scheduling season[a]
Authorization to buy or sell slots	Allowed	Not authorized	Not authorized	Not authorized
Authorization to lease or trade slots	Allowed	Allowed	Allowed	Allowed

Source: FAA and FAA regulations

[a]Slots that are not operated because the airline returned them to FAA prior to that season's return deadline are not counted as unused for purposes of measuring slot usage. Airlines can return to FAA slots during periods of a season that the airline does not intend to operate.

According to FAA officials, the differences in the rules for each airport are largely a product of history. For example, when FAA replaced the High Density Rule with temporary limitations on flight operations at LaGuardia in 2007, it adopted most of the rule's provisions including, most importantly, the slot caps. Long-term changes were expected through a proposed rule issued by FAA in the summer of 2006. Additionally, according to an FAA official and International Air Transport Association (IATA) representatives, because JFK and Newark support a large number of international operations, the rules for those airports are more consistent with IATA's Worldwide Slot Guidelines. These guidelines contain slot processes and policies for slot-controlled airports to facilitate international operations to or between other slot-controlled airports around the world.

FAA and DOT's Office of the Secretary share responsibility for managing slot control issues. FAA is responsible for administering the slot rules, which primarily includes slot allocation, transfers, and monitoring and enforcing airlines' compliance with the 80 percent slot usage requirement. DOT's Office of the Secretary is responsible for awarding within-perimeter and beyond-perimeter slot exemptions at Reagan National and monitoring competitive aspects of the airlines' slot holdings.

In 2006, FAA proposed a congestion management rule for LaGuardia that would limit operations, encourage the use of larger aircraft, and assign rolling expiration dates for slots. That notice of proposed rulemaking was withdrawn and superseded in 2008 by congestion management rules at JFK, LaGuardia, and Newark that would have created a market by annually auctioning a limited number of slots in each of the first 5 years of the rule, which had a 10-year term. In October 2009, before the terms of the 2008 rules became effective, FAA rescinded the rules citing, among other things, that the rulemakings had been highly controversial, and a court challenge that resulted in a December 2008 stay of the rules by the United States Court of Appeals for the District of Columbia Circuit. In addition, because of the complexity of the issues, the impact of an Omnibus Appropriations Act, 2009 provision,[15] and the possible impact of the significantly changed economic circumstances on the slot auction program, FAA believed it was better to rescind the rule rather than propose to extend it.

According to DOT's Office of the Secretary and FAA, their Slot and Management Transparency notice of proposed rulemaking currently being drafted will propose to replace the current temporary orders limiting scheduled operations at JFK, LaGuardia, and Newark with a permanent rule to address congestion and delay, while also promoting fair access and competition, including establishing a secondary market that would allow airlines to buy and sell slots at the New York City area airports.[16]

In 2009, because airlines are prohibited from selling or purchasing slots under the temporary order at LaGuardia, Delta Air Lines and US Airways sought a waiver from DOT's Office of the Secretary and FAA from this prohibition to exchange slots at LaGuardia and Reagan National because Delta wanted to establish a domestic hub at LaGuardia and US Airways wanted to increase service at Reagan National. In 2011, DOT's Office of the Secretary and FAA together granted the joint waiver request that permitted the transfer and sale of more than 300 slots between the two airlines, provided that they divest a total of 48 slots (24 slot pairs) at Reagan National and LaGuardia to new airline entrants and airlines holding less than 5 percent of the slots at those airports.

After the slot swap, Delta Air Lines increased its share of slot holdings at LaGuardia from 24 percent in April 2011 to 44 percent in May 2012 and US Airways increased its share of slot holdings at Reagan National from 31 percent in April 2011 to 54 percent in May 2012. The divestiture effort, conducted through a blind sale open to new entrants and limited incumbents only, resulted in JetBlue attaining 16 slots at LaGuardia for $32 million and 16 slots at Reagan National for $40 million, and WestJet attaining 16 slots at LaGuardia for $17.6 million. Under the terms of the slot swap, US Airways and Delta were to receive the proceeds from the sale of their divested slots.

DOJ is responsible for enforcing antitrust laws for most sectors of the economy, including the airline industry. According to DOJ officials, this includes reviewing competitive aspects of airlines' holdings at slot-controlled airports. For example, transactions that increase concentration of slot holdings may substantially lessen competition in violation of the antitrust laws. In 2010, DOJ offered formal comments in support of the tentative decision by DOT's Office of the Secretary and FAA to condition approval of the slots transfer between Delta Air Lines and US Airways with regard to the airlines' slot holdings at LaGuardia and Reagan National on the airlines divesting a certain number of slots. While DOJ did not take action to block the slot swap, DOJ officials told us in June 2012 that they are still reviewing competitive aspects of the airlines' slot holdings at Reagan National following completion of the revised slot swap.

In addition to slot controls, Reagan National and LaGuardia are subject to perimeter rules, which limit nonstop flights serving these airports to a distance of 1,250 and 1,500 miles,[17] respectively. While LaGuardia's perimeter rule is imposed by the airport's operator, the perimeter rule at Reagan National is statutory.[18] Two federal laws—the Wendell H. Ford Aviation Investment and Reform Act for the 21st Century (AIR-21)[19] in 2000 and the Vision 100-Century of Aviation Reauthorization Act (Vision 100)[20] in 2003—increased the number of slot exemptions at Reagan National and for the first time required exemptions to be granted to the Reagan National perimeter rule known as "beyond-perimeter" slot exemptions. These laws required the Secretary of Transportation to grant exemptions to the existing rules, adding 44 slot exemption operations (22 round trips) per day during a 15-hour period and requiring 24 (12 round trips) of these slot exemptions to be granted for beyond-perimeter flights.[21] In February 2012, the FAA Modernization and Reform Act of 2012[22] required the Secretary of Transportation to grant 8 additional beyond-perimeter slots exemptions (4 round trips) at Reagan National.

The 2012 act, similar to AIR-21 in 2000 and Vision 100 in 2003, required DOT, in awarding the slot exemptions, to consider specified criteria in granting beyond-perimeter exemptions. The 2012 act required the consideration of issues such as their impact on providing network benefits (connecting flights) outside of the perimeter and passenger service to small communities.

In May 2012, to implement the requirements of the FAA Modernization and Reform Act, DOT awarded the beyond-perimeter slot exemptions to airlines proposing to provide nonstop service between Reagan National and Austin, Texas; Portland, Oregon; San Francisco, California; and San Juan, Puerto Rico. The act also authorized the four incumbent carriers at Reagan National to each convert two slots that were being used for flights to large hubs within the perimeter, to two slot exemptions for nonstop flights beyond the perimeter. Accordingly, four round trips were suspended to large hubs and four new round trips were initiated instead to Los Angeles, San Diego, and San Francisco, California, and Salt Lake City, Utah (using a total of eight slot exemptions) (see fig. 2).

Appendix III provides more detailed information about the implementation of slot controls and perimeter rules, the proposed Slot Management and Transparency rule, and the slots transfer between Delta Air Lines and US Airways.

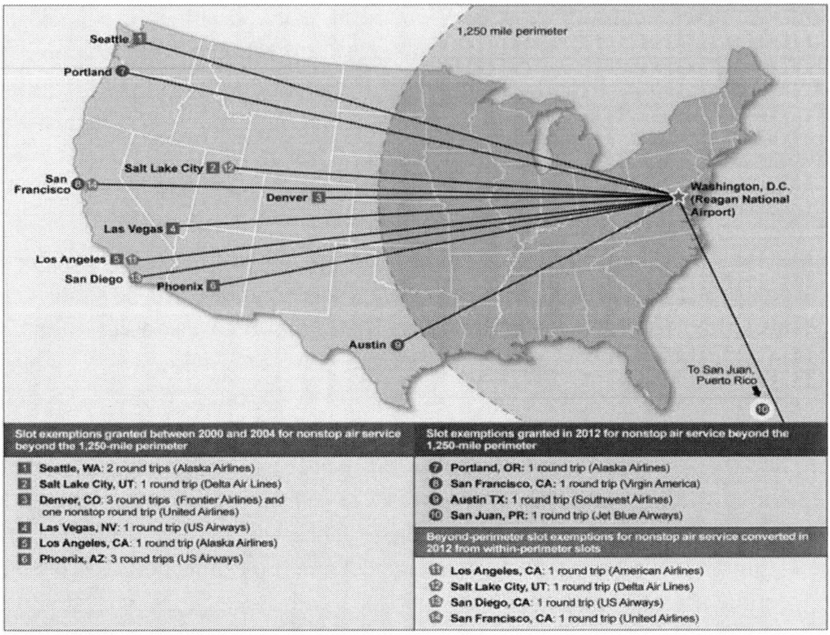

Source: DOT and Map Resources.

Figure 2. Nonstop Beyond-Perimeter Slot Exemption Destinations from Reagan National from 2000 through 2012.

REAGAN NATIONAL CAN ACCOMMODATE NEW BEYOND-PERIMETER FLIGHTS, WHICH ARE LIKELY TO HAVE A LIMITED EFFECT ON OTHER WASHINGTON, D.C., AREA AIRPORTS

Reagan National has sufficient airside (runway) capacity to accommodate the new nonstop beyond-perimeter flights. The airport's terminal and landside facilities are more constrained, but with some improvements and adjustments, it will also have sufficient terminal capacity. The new flights are also likely to have limited effects on passenger security screening wait times, passenger traffic at the other Washington, D.C., area airports, MWAA's ability to service its debt, and aircraft noise. In addition, the low cost airlines that will be operating half of the new beyond-perimeter flights at Reagan National will increase airline competition on those routes.

Table 2. Hourly Aircraft Operations (Takeoffs and Landings) Allowed at Reagan National

Type of aircraft operations	Maximum number of takeoffs andlandings (slots) allowed per hour
Air carrier[a]	37
Commuter aircraft operations[b]	11
General aviation and unscheduled flights	12
Slot exemptions[c]	5
Slides[d](allowing slots to be used in different time periods)	2
Total[e]	67

Source: 14 C.F.R. § 93.123, 49 U.S.C. § 41718(c)(2)(A)(ii), 49 U.S.C. § 41714(d)(1) and FAA.

[a]Under FAA slot control regulations applicable to Reagan National, "air carrier slots" are intended for operations with turboprop and reciprocating engine aircraft with 75 or more seats or turbojet aircraft with 56 or more seats. However, air carrier slots may be used for operations using aircraft of any size. FAA officials estimated that 30 to 40 percent of air carrier slots are operated in commuter aircraft slots based on a review of published schedules and the number of commuter aircraft operated above the commuter slot quota.

[b]Under FAA slot control regulations applicable to Reagan National, "commuter slots" may be used only for operations with turboprop and reciprocating engine aircraft with no more than 76 seats or turbojet aircraft with fewer than 56 seats.

[c]These are exemptions to the hourly restrictions at Reagan National that are authorized by statute.

[d]Under 49 U.S.C. § 41714 (d)(1), the Secretary of Transportation is authorized to grant certain exemptions from specified slot rules applicable to Reagan National. For example, under this authority the Secretary may grant exemptions from hourly limitations on slots at Reagan National but may not increase the number of aircraft operations in any 1-hour period by more than 2 operations. FAA may not grant more than 2 exemptions for a 1-hour period. FAA uses this authority to consider requests for what are referred to as a grant "slot-slides," which would allow slots allocated for certain hours to be reassigned and used in a different slot periods.

[e]Regulatory limits are 60 per hour. However, slot exemptions are authorized by statute to increase hourly operations by up to 5 in an hour, but only between 7:00 a.m. and 9:59 p.m. In addition, slot slides may also increase operations but under statute (1) may not result in an increase in the total number of slots per day, (2) may not result in an increase in the total number of slots from 7:00 a.m. to 9:00 p.m., and (3) may not increase operations in any 1-hour period by more than two operations. FAA has not modeled the delay impact of 67 operations in each hour.

Airside Capacity

Reagan National is routinely operating below the maximum authorized 67 hourly takeoffs and landings (slots) and the 67.6 hourly takeoffs and landings that a 2011 FAA capacity analysis indicated could be accommodated based only on average runway capacity.[23] While 67 is the maximum number of hourly takeoffs and landings authorized in any one hour, the number of slots and slot exemptions authorized on a daily basis is generally less than 67 per hour, on average. Table 2 shows the maximum number of hourly takeoffs and landings allowed at Reagan National, broken down by the type of aircraft operations. Our analysis of FAA data found that a maximum of about 53 slots was allocated and used per hour at Reagan National, compared with the 67 hourly takeoffs and landings that are generally permitted. Specifically, FAA reported that a maximum of 52 slots in one hour was allocated for airline and commuter operations in April 2012 and an average of about 1 aircraft operation per hour was used for general aviation or unscheduled aircraft operations from May through August 2011.[24] The new beyond-perimeter flights will cause the largest increase in the maximum number of slot allocations for airline and commuter aircraft operations from 4:00 p.m. to 6:59 p.m., when the number of slot allocations will increase by 2 per hour.[25] Table 3 shows the impact of the new beyond-perimeter flights on slot allocations during peak and nonpeak hours.

Table 3. Impact of New Beyond-Perimeter Exemptions on Average Peak and Non-Peak Hour Slot Allocations at Reagan National for the Summer 2012 Season

Type of aircraft operations	Average number of slots allocated per hour during peak hours[a]	Average number of slots allocated per hour during peak hours[a] including the new beyond-perimeter flights[b]	Average number of slots allocated per hour during nonpeak hours	Average number of slotsallocated per hour duringnonpeak hours includingthe new beyond-perimeterflights[b]
Airline and commuter operations[c]	51.3	52.5	45.6	45.7

Source: GAO analysis of FAA data.

[a]Peak hours used in this analysis are from 7:00 a.m. to 10:00 a.m. and from 4:00 p.m. to 7:00 p.m. [b]New beyond-perimeter slots that Congress authorized in February 2012.

[c]Based on FAA data regarding slot holders for Thursdays for the summer 2012 season as of April 5, 2012.

Much of the difference between the maximum number of hourly aircraft operations authorized and the average number of slots allocated and used can be attributed to a substantial decrease in general aviation and unscheduled aircraft operations at Reagan National after the September 11, 2001, terrorist attacks. After the 2001 terrorist attacks, TSA imposed security restrictions on general aviation operations operating at Reagan National, such as requiring an armed security officer to be on board all flights. Before the attacks, there were about 210 general aviation and unscheduled flights per day at Reagan National. By comparison, FAA indicated that there were about 17 general aviation and unscheduled flights per day at Reagan National in 2011.[26] Of the 60 authorized hourly slots at Reagan National, excluding any slot exemptions, 12 are allocated for general aviation aircraft operations or other aircraft that do not operate on a scheduled basis. However, from May through August 2011, an average of about 1 of the 12 allocated slots was used per hour. Although airlines with large commercial aircraft could not necessarily use the slots reserved for smaller general aviation aircraft and unscheduled flights, which may use the airport's shorter runways and do not generally use airport gates and terminal infrastructure, the reduced amount of overall general aviation traffic leaves some airport capacity unused. In addition, some slots are available at Reagan National during nonpeak hours because airlines are primarily interested in obtaining slots at peak hours. FAA indicated that, for July and August 2012, 34 airline and 12 commuter slots were available, all at early morning (6:00 a.m.) or late evening (10:00 p.m. or 11:00 p.m.) hours.[27]

Terminal Capacity

Although Reagan National has sufficient airside capacity to accommodate the new beyond-perimeter flights, the airport has more limited terminal capacity, which includes space for gates, ticket counters, baggage handling, and security screening. As of May 2012, two of the new beyond-perimeter round trips (those operated by Jet Blue and Southwest Airlines) are expected to be operated out of Terminal A, the airport's original terminal that opened in 1941, and two of the new beyond-perimeter round trips (those operated by Virgin America, which is the airport's only new airline entrant among the operators of the new beyond-perimeter flights, and Alaska Airlines) are expected to be operated out of the newer Terminal B/C, which opened in 1997. To help accommodate as many as 1,245 additional daily passengers who could fly on the new beyond-perimeter flights, MWAA is planning to expand baggage and security screening space in Terminal A and complete those improvements by the summer of 2013. An MWAA official said these improvements were already needed to address increased passenger volume and complexity of operations in Terminal A. For example, seven airlines, each with its own needs for space in Terminal A,[28] are now operating separate, uncoordinated schedules, compared with a few years ago when one dominant airline and a few smaller airlines were operating there. No improvements will be needed to accommodate the new beyond-perimeter flights in Terminal B/C. MWAA estimated that improvements in Terminal A will cost about $45.6 million, which will be financed through bond funds and airline leases. However, an MWAA official added that these improvements do not allow for any additional growth in Terminal A, which could, if needed, require replacing the terminal at a cost of several hundred million dollars.

Gate Usage

Based on current gate usage rates at Reagan National, on average, gates will be fully used. MWAA data indicated that airlines operating at Reagan National will average 7.7 turns per day for each gate. This is in the range of six to eight daily turns per gate that was defined as full gate utilization in a 2010 Transportation Research Board study[29] on common-use gates. That report also indicated that full gate utilization may be affected by noise restrictions limiting the hours of operations or other factors that may vary according to the airline using the gate. Exceeding full gate utilization could lead to flight delays.

Passenger Security Screening

We asked TSA to estimate the impact of the new beyond-perimeter flights on passenger security screening wait times at Reagan National using the agency's security screening throughput model. TSA's model suggested that the impact of the new beyond-perimeter flights on passenger security screening wait times would be minimal.[30] However, an MWAA official said that until improvements to the security screening space in Terminal A are completed next summer, passengers may need to wait longer to be screened at that checkpoint.

Airport Access and Parking

The additional beyond-perimeter flights are not expected to affect access to the airport or parking, considering that the maximum number of additional passengers that the new flights could generate represents about 5 percent of the airport's total daily enplanements. According to a survey of air passengers in the Washington, D.C., and Baltimore area, 16 percent of Reagan National passengers arrive by Metrorail, which is among the highest public transportation rates in the nation for airport access, 74 percent of passengers arrive by car (private and rental) or taxi, and the remaining 10 percent arrive by shuttle bus or Metrobus.[31] MWAA provided data showing that since parking facilities were expanded since 2009, the number of times that lots have been filled to capacity has dropped considerably. The data indicated that in 2011, the airport's parking lots were filled to capacity approximately 38 times, compared with 2009, when they were filled to capacity a total of 353 times. According to MWAA, from January through May 2012, the parking lots were filled to capacity 13 times. However, an MWAA official said that the impact of the new beyond-perimeter slot exemptions should not be considered in isolation and that the sale of slots to JetBlue under the Delta-US Airways slots swap earlier in 2011 has had a more pronounced effect. For example, the official said that since more JetBlue flights began operating out of Terminal A in June 2012, the economy parking lot has been filled to capacity an average of 4 days a week. In providing comments on a draft of this report, MWAA indicated that during the first 8 months of 2012, the economy parking lot has been filled to capacity more than 60 times, which was more than double the number of times that the lot was forced to close in 2011.

Impact on Other Airports in the Washington, D.C., Area

Our analysis found that the beyond-perimeter flights authorized in February 2012 could add between zero (assuming that no new passengers shift from using other airports) and a maximum of 1,245 daily enplanements (departing passengers) at Reagan National.[32] Longstanding policy designed to guide the operation of Reagan National and Dulles, as well as agency rules designed to implement such policy, have included the roles of Reagan National in providing short-haul domestic service and Dulles in providing all types of service.[33] In addition, under the policy, MWAA is to promote the "better utilization" of Dulles, which was underutilized for many years after opening in 1962. During our review, MWAA and BWI officials expressed concern about the possible impact of the new beyond-perimeter flights at Reagan National on passenger traffic at Dulles and BWI. We found, on the basis of 2011 enplanement data, that if all of the new beyond-perimeter flights are 100 percent full, the number of enplanements on those flights would represent an increase of about 5 percent of annual enplanements at Reagan National. Correspondingly, Dulles or BWI would lose a maximum of 4.1 percent of their enplanements, respectively, if all the passengers changed from using either of these two airports to using Reagan National. Therefore, if all the passengers changed from using Dulles or BWI, the new beyond-perimeter flights are likely to have some impact on passenger traffic at these airports. However, it is extremely unlikely that all of these passengers would shift from using one airport; instead, any loss likely would be shared between Dulles and BWI. In addition, the airports are not perfect substitutes for Reagan National, so it is unlikely that all the passenger traffic would shift from Dulles or BWI. But, even in the worst case, a 4.1 percent change is less than the growth expected at these airports over the next 2 or 3 years. The actual impact of the new beyond-perimeter flights at Reagan National on passenger traffic at the other Washington, D.C., area airports cannot be quantified because all of the new flights did not start until August 2012 and because of unknown factors such as how competing flights will be priced, how the new direct flights at Reagan National will draw passengers from the area airports, how other airlines may adjust their schedules, and the extent to which the new flights may generate new passenger demand on those routes.

We found no evidence that the previously added beyond-perimeter flights at Reagan National had affected passenger traffic or airfares at the surrounding airports. We found two cases—one in 2005 and another in 2012[34]—when airlines discontinued or planned to discontinue service between Dulles and beyond-perimeter destinations after they were awarded new beyond-perimeter slot exemptions at Reagan National, but any shift in passenger traffic, as noted above, represented about 4 percent of overall passenger traffic. (Figures 8 through 31 in appendix IV show trends in average annual passenger traffic and airfares at BWI and Dulles for destinations granted beyond-perimeter slot exemptions at Reagan National under AIR-21 and Vision 100 between 2000 and 2004). Moreover, any deviation in airfares after the initiation of the slot exemptions at Reagan National could be a result of many factors, such as airline bankruptcies and mergers. Additionally, the presence of low cost airlines on the newly-awarded beyond-perimeter flights will increase competition on those routes and could help reduce airfares to those destinations. However, of the four new nonstop beyond-perimeter destinations, only one low cost airline (Virgin America) will be competing with a legacy airline (United Airlines) in providing service between Reagan National and San Francisco.

Financial Impact on MWAA

If the new beyond-perimeter flights cause passengers to shift from using Dulles to using Reagan National, it could increase per passenger airline costs of using Dulles, which, if substantial, could cause the airlines to reduce service at the airport. To better understand the potential financial impact of possible changes in passenger traffic resulting from the new beyond-perimeter exemptions, we asked MWAA to estimate the flights' impact on the cost per enplaned passenger,[35] which is a generalized measure of airline's airport charges, assuming a worst case scenario.

Table 4. Projected Impact of the New Beyond-Perimeter Flights at Reagan National on the Cost per Enplaned Passenger in 2013 and 2014

Airport	Projected 2013 cost per enplaned passenger	Projected 2013 cost per enplaned passenger with new beyond-perimeter flights	Projected 2014 cost per enplaned passenger	Projected 2014 cost perenplaned passenger withnew beyond-perimeterflights
Reagan National	\$13.23[a]	\$12.65	\$13.70[b]	\$12.81
Dulles	\$27.99[c]	\$29.09	\$26.61[d]	\$28.12

Source: MWAA

[a]Based on projected enplanements of 9,765,000. [b]Based on projected enplanements of 9,850,000. [c]Based on projected enplanements of 12,095,000. [d]Based on projected enplanements of 12,415,000.

Assuming all of the passengers on the new beyond-perimeter flights shifted from using Dulles to using Reagan National—the worst case scenario—and all other factors stayed the same, MWAA's analysis found that the cost per enplaned passenger would increase at Dulles in 2013 by \$1.10, or 3.9 percent, and increase in 2014 by \$1.51 or 5.7 percent, and decrease at Reagan National in 2013 by \$0.58, or 4.4 percent, and decrease in 2014 by \$0.89, or 6.5 percent (see table 4). These results show that because the same costs, most of which are fixed costs, would be spread among fewer passengers at Dulles and more at Reagan National so that the cost per enplaned passenger would change accordingly. However, even in the worst case, the changes would be relatively small.

In recent years, the cost per enplaned passenger has increased substantially at Dulles, owing to a major capital development project at the airport, while it has decreased slightly at Reagan National. From 2010 to the first half of 2012, the cost per enplaned passenger at Dulles increased from $17.16 to $26.03 or 51.7 percent, but decreased at Reagan National from $12.84 to $12.74, or 0.8 percent. Airline representatives generally told us that an airport's cost as measured by cost per enplaned passenger is among many factors that they consider when deciding whether to provide service there. However, representatives from one large airline said that if the cost per enplaned passenger at Dulles and other costs such as fuel continue to increase, it would consider reducing or cancelling its service there. MWAA officials also said that, given the recent substantial increases in the cost per enplaned passenger at Dulles, some airlines may stop serving the airport, particularly in providing domestic service, and that an increase of even one dollar in the cost per enplaned passenger is significant.[36] In a recent credit-rating report on MWAA prepared in September 2011, before the new beyond-perimeter flights were awarded, one agency had a negative outlook on the authority's rating because of expected significant increases in the cost per enplaned passenger and lower debt service coverage over the next 5 years. However, two other credit-rating agencies reported in September 2011 their ratings outlooks for MWAA were stable, citing the strong air passenger market in the Washington, D.C., area. Moreover, recent increases in the cost per enplaned passenger at Dulles were not due to significant shifts in passenger traffic. From 2010 through 2011, enplanements at Dulles decreased by about 2 percent, while they increased at Reagan National by about 3.6 percent. However, from 2010 and 2011, international enplanements—which generate higher airport revenues because airline fees are based in part on aircraft weight, and aircraft used for international flights are generally larger and heavier— increased at Dulles by more than 4 percent and represented 28 percent of all enplanements in 2011. In addition, in a forecast of airport activity from 2011 to 2040, FAA ranked Dulles second among 30 major U.S. airports in terms of projected increases in enplanements, with a projected annual growth rate of 3.9 percent. FAA projected that from 2011 to 2040, enplanements at Dulles will increase by 215 percent, compared with 34 percent at Reagan National and 110 percent at BWI.[37]

Under current lease agreements between MWAA and its incumbent airlines, debt costs are not shared between the two airports which could make servicing the much larger debt at Dulles difficult if revenue declines at Dulles were substantial. MWAA currently maintains $5.2 billion in longterm debt. [38] Much of MWAA's debt was incurred for recent major capital improvements at Dulles, such as an automated train system[39] connecting the main terminal to gates and construction of a fourth runway. According to an MWAA official, about $3.8 billion of the $5.2 billion in total debt is allocated to Dulles and about $1.4 billion is allocated to Reagan National.[40] MWAA officials are concerned about the financial impact of the new beyond-perimeter flights on the authority's ability to service its debt at Dulles, because revenues and debt service charges for Reagan National and Dulles are maintained separately.[41] According to MWAA officials, in the event that one of the two airports could not pay its debt, the lease agreements contain an "extraordinary coverage protection payments" provision designed to allow for the sharing of debt service between the two airports. More specifically, according to MWAA officials, if Dulles could not continue paying its debt service, the use of the extraordinary coverage provision by the authority could have the impact of mitigating airline rates and charges at Dulles and, in turn, could mitigate a cost per enplaned passenger increase at Dulles and cause a corresponding increase in the cost per enplaned passenger at Reagan National. However, an MWAA official said that the airports authority does not expect that this provision will be triggered before the current lease agreements expire in the fall of 2014. In addition, the MWAA official said the inclusion of this provision in the new leases is a matter that will be negotiated with the airlines.

With respect to MWAA's authority to generate additional revenues that could help mitigate the cost per enplaned passenger in the future, the FAA Modernization and Reform Act of 2012 amended the definition of the "airport purposes" that MWAA may engage in to include "a business or activity not inconsistent with the needs of aviation that has been approved by the Secretary."[42] An MWAA official said that, pursuant to this authority, the airport authority plans to develop land near Dulles for warehouses, cargo-related integrators, freight forwarders, and general aviation. However, the official added that the property first needs to undergo an environmental impact review, which could take 2 to 3 years, and that new revenues from the development are not expected to have an impact on airline lease rates in the next 3 to 7 years.

Aircraft Noise

Although some members of the community surrounding Reagan National expressed limited concerns about the additional aircraft noise that the new beyond-perimeter flights could generate, FAA and airport officials indicated that the relatively small number of flights being added will not have a significant overall effect on aircraft noise. Concerns about noise affecting nearby residential areas were a primary reason why Reagan National became subject to the perimeter rule in the 1960s, when aircraft were noisier than they are today. We interviewed individuals from community organizations concerned about aircraft noise at Reagan National as well as officials from the Washington Council of Governments, the Arlington County (Va.) Council, MWAA, and FAA about the possible impact on aircraft noise from the new beyond-perimeter flights. Individuals from community organizations said they were concerned about aircraft noise at the airport as a whole and that continuing to add more beyond-perimeter flights has a cumulative negative effect. The Washington Council of Governments opposed changing the slot or perimeter rules at Reagan National, which the organization indicated are important tools in helping to manage the volume of air traffic at the airport and the impact on aircraft noise on the surrounding community. In addition, the Arlington County Council official said that people would notice noise from the new flights if they were added in the early morning or late evening hours. However, MWAA and FAA officials said that the additional beyond-perimeter flights are not expected to cause a noticeable increase in aircraft noise because they constitute only 8 of about 800 daily flights at Reagan National, or about 1 percent, of the total daily aircraft operations. They also noted that aircraft make less noise than they did in the past and that the types of aircraft being used or planned to be used for the new beyond-perimeter flights (Airbus 319s and 320s and Boeing 737s) tend to be newer and quieter. An MWAA noise abatement official also said and that in February 2012, a new advanced navigational procedure was implemented for northbound departures at Reagan National, which is designed for aircraft to follow the river and fly less directly over homes. FAA and MWAA officials also said that because of the technological advances, noise contours, which highlight areas of significant aircraft noise exposure surrounding the airport, have generally shrunk and that while noise from the new beyond-perimeter flights would be noticeable individually, the relatively small number of new beyond-perimeter flights being added as a whole is not significant enough to require updating the airport's noise compatibility study.[43]

MWAA, which monitors noise at Reagan National, provided data showing that in 2011, it received 505 complaints from 117 callers, 255 of which came from 5 callers, compared with 197 complaints in 2010 and 99 complaints in 2009. An MWAA official attributed the increased number of complaints to construction on the main runway last year, which is now complete. During construction, pilots took a different flight path over residential areas at night, rather than following the normal path along the Potomac River.

SLOT CONTROL RULES HELP MANAGE CONGESTION, BUT ALLOWING AIRLINES NOT TO USE SOME SLOTS MAY HINDER COMPETITION

Slot Control Rules Help FAA Manage Congestion

Even though the New York City area airports still experience some of the worst delays in the country, the delay situation at these airports would be far worse in the absence of slot controls.[44] The best example of what would occur without slot controls at New York City area airports occurred in 2000 when a then-new federal law required the Secretary of Transportation to grant exemptions to the High Density Rule at JFK and LaGuardia to new entrant airlines and for service to small communities with small regional jets.[45] Soon after, qualifying airlines requested more than 600 new slot exemptions at LaGuardia and by September 2000, 25 percent of the flight delays in the United States were attributed to congestion at LaGuardia. FAA reports that after it again capped the number of scheduled takeoffs and landings at LaGuardia in 2001, aircraft delays of 15 minutes or more fell from 330 per day in October 2000 to 98 per day in April 2001.[46] In setting operating limits at JFK and Newark in 2008, FAA conducted analyses with the goal of reducing average departure delays at JFK by about 15 percent compared with their 2007 level, and to keep delays at Newark from increasing above their 2007 level.[47] Airline representatives with whom we spoke mostly agreed that some form of slot controls are needed at the four airports to manage congestion. However, representatives from two airlines believed that if slot controls were lifted, congestion initially would spike, but airlines would eventually make the adjustments needed to reach a level of manageable congestion.

Despite Demand for Additional Slots at Slot- Controlled Airports, Some Slots Go Unused While Others Are Underutilized

Existing slot control rules require airlines to operate their slots at least 80 percent of the time, which allows airlines to not schedule some of their allocated slots. FAA has interpreted the rules to allow airlines to apply the usage requirement across a pool of slots they hold within a slot period— an allowance that provides an advantage to airlines with large slot holdings in meeting the usage requirement. Further, FAA's current process for overseeing airlines' compliance of the 80 percent slot usage requirement, including its recordkeeping, does not provide sufficient assurance that it can adequately identify instances when airlines do not meet the 80 percent slot usage requirement. We also found that airlines tend to underutilize the slots they do operate at slot-controlled airports as compared with like-sized airports that are not slot-controlled.[48] Specifically, flights operated at slot-controlled airports tend to use smaller aircraft and are on average less full, which means that fewer passengers are served then would be otherwise.

Unused Capacity

Available airport capacity at slot controlled airports can go unused in three distinct ways. The first of these are slots that are unallocated (i.e., slots that are not currently held by any airline). These slots, however, are generally at times of day that airlines find undesirable, such as early morning or late evening slots. Although unallocated slots go unused, they are available for any airline to request and operate.[49] Second, some additional amount of available capacity goes unused because airlines do not schedule all of the slots that they are allocated. Third, more capacity goes unused because airlines do not operate all of the flights that they schedule, although this is in part because of cancellations resulting from unforeseeable circumstances.[50] As discussed below, we could not calculate precisely how much capacity is unused among these three levels or even overall because current airline reporting and FAA recordkeeping do not allow these calculations. Figure 3 illustrates the three areas in which capacity can go unused at slot-controlled airports. The amount that goes unused varies depending on the airport, airline, time of year, and demand for air travel.

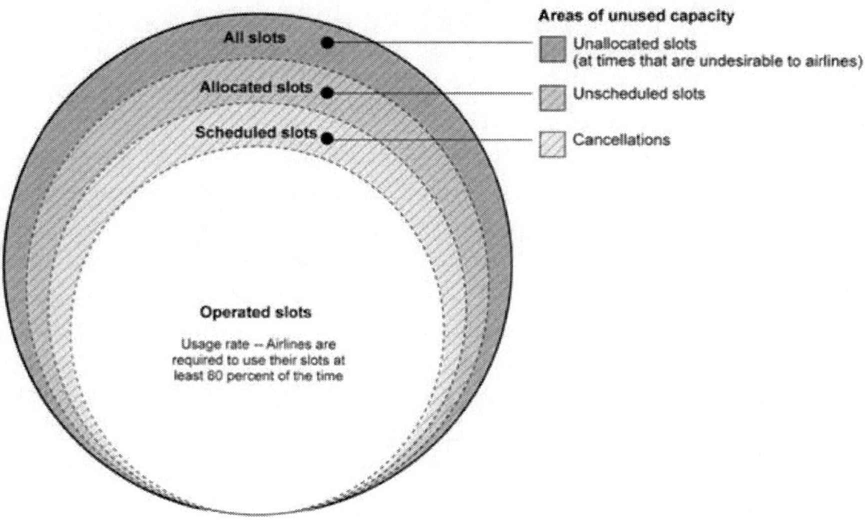

Source: GAO.

Figure 3. Areas of Unused Capacity at Slot-Controlled Airports.

Unscheduled Slots

Although slot control rules require airlines to operate their slots at least 80 percent of the time, or the slots are subject to withdrawal by FAA, the rules do not require a minimum level for which the airlines must schedule their slots. Therefore, the usage requirement allows airlines to not schedule or to suspend flights for operational reasons (such as cancellations because of bad weather or ground delays) up to 20 percent of the time.[51] According to FAA officials, it is not the agency's intention for airlines to operate at the minimum usage rate of 80 percent because unforeseen circumstances would result in the airline losing their slots.

Generally, airlines consider slots that they hold to be valuable assets, in part, because slots are a scarce resource that allows airlines to operate flights at airports with a high demand for air travel.[52] However, airlines may not need all of their allocated slots at a point in time. Even so, airlines still have an incentive to hold onto their slots, even if that means leasing them, because if they return them to FAA the slots could be reallocated to a competitor. During our review, we found that airlines at U.S. slot-controlled airports are not scheduling all of their allocated slots. Specifically, our analysis of aggregated airline schedules for certain days in 2011, indicated that generally airlines in aggregate scheduled between 80 percent and 100 percent of their slot allocations (depending on the airport, day of week, and season), but on specific days, one or more airlines scheduled as little as 75 percent of all daily allocated slots.[53] Because slot usage is measured across multiple days of a reporting period—all days within a 2-month period at Reagan National and LaGuardia and each day of the week within a season for JFK and Newark—airlines can schedule less than 80 percent of their allocated slots on a single day and still meet the 80 percent usage requirement.

Internationally, where slot controls are more prevalent than in the United States, airlines generally schedule all of their slots. IATA representatives told us that airlines operating at slot-controlled airports outside of the United States generally schedule 100 percent of their allocated slots and that it may be seen as abuse if they don't schedule all of their slots. Under the Worldwide Slot Guidelines, airlines may only hold slots that they intend to operate, transfer, exchange or use in a shared operation, and violations are subject to sanction under local regulation or national law. FAA, however, in implementing U.S. slot control rules, generally does not calculate or know airlines' schedule rates. Requiring airlines to schedule all of their slots could encourage airlines to sell or lease slots to airlines that desire them or return slots to FAA that they do not intend to use, but it could also cause airlines to operate more flights than necessary to meet demand for routes within their business model as a means of meeting the 80 percent usage requirement. Airlines would only operate additional flights, though, if the perceived cost of relinquishing their slot—such as the risk of a competitor operating the slot—is higher than the cost they would incur from operating the flight.

Slot Usage Rate Compliance

FAA's current process for overseeing airlines' compliance of the 80 percent slot usage requirement, including its recordkeeping, does not provide sufficient assurance that it can adequately identify instances when airlines do not meet the 80 percent slot usage requirement. FAA uses a slot management system to compile usage data reported by airlines and validate that data against FAA's slot allocation records. FAA then reviews instances of potential noncompliance on an exception basis—that is, FAA reviews only those instances that its system identifies as below the 80 percent slot usage rate. Our review of FAA's process for overseeing airlines' slot usage, combined with FAA's inability to provide documentation verifying airlines' compliance with the usage requirement and our limited analysis of FAA aggregated data on airlines' flight schedules and slot allocation records, raised questions regarding

FAA's ability to effectively identify instances of noncompliance. Issues we identified include the following.

- Usage rates are generally not calculated: At the end of each reporting period, airlines submit reports to FAA that include the minimum required data for each slot, including whether the slot was operated, the flight number, and the scheduled time of departure, but do not include actual usage rates. FAA officials said that they do not calculate the actual slot usage rate for each airline's slot holdings, in part, because the format in which airlines report the data makes it difficult to correlate the slots to the flights that were operated. For example, flights operated by Airline A using slots leased or exchanged from Airline B may be reported by Airline A, but would need to be considered in Airline B's usage rate but not in Airline A's rate. The airline reports generally do not make this distinction. Furthermore, FAA does not require airlines to report the same flight in a specific slot throughout the reporting period, which further complicates FAA's ability to correlate a slot to the flight that was operated. Without calculating airlines' actual usage rate, FAA does not know precisely how much available capacity goes unused, which hinders its ability to manage slots and the airspace.
- Reliance on self-reported data in a variety of formats: Instead of calculating the actual usage rate, FAA compares airlines' reported data with FAA slot allocation records and in so doing will correct discrepancies or errors. However, FAA does not fully verify the accuracy of airlines' self-reported data. Furthermore, FAA does not require a specific format for airlines' usage reports. Therefore, some reports are received in a database format that can be entered into FAA's slot management system through an automated interface. Others require FAA to manually enter data from a spreadsheet into its system. In some cases, FAA officials told us that if extensive reporting errors or formatting or other administrative changes are needed, they may require the airline to submit a supplemental or corrected usage report.
- Limitations in FAA's database: Because of the difficulties in calculating usage rates by FAA, we conducted a limited analysis of airline schedule data and FAA data to assess the extent to which airlines were using their slots. Using slot allocation records for scheduled passenger flights provided by FAA for select days and

matching them against airline flight schedules for those days, we examined the extent to which airlines were scheduling their slots. Based on our initial analysis, we determined that in one instance at least one airline had not met the 80 percent usage requirement at Newark.[54] Although our method of analysis is not the method that FAA uses to oversee individual airlines' compliance with the usage requirement, FAA officials agreed that our method could be used to assess whether some of the slots were, at times, operated less than 80 percent of the time. Our method would not gauge individual airline's compliance, but would provide an aggregated check of usage by all airlines. FAA officials told us that they were not aware of the problem at Newark so they rechecked their slot allocation records and realized that the total slot allocation numbers in their data for Newark and JFK were inaccurate. Specifically, their records did not account for slots that airlines "handback" (i.e., return) to FAA prior to the slot's handback deadline. Airlines at Newark and JFK are allowed to and routinely do return to FAA blocks of slots (e.g., specific days of the week or short periods of time) that they initially requested and were allocated by FAA but do not intend to operate during the season.[55] FAA officials said that they do not always update their slot allocation database with the lists of returned slots because it would be too resource-intensive and because of limitations in the computer software. While removing the handbacks from the allocation numbers provided to us increased the airlines' presumed usage rate above 80 percent at Newark airport, FAA did not calculate the usage rates with the corrected data and thus, could not provide us verification that the airlines usage exceeded 80 percent. And, it does not remove our concerns regarding the accuracy of FAA's data or process for verifying compliance with the 80 percent rule.

- Slot trades and leases: FAA's review is further complicated by the number and frequency of slot trades and leases between airlines. FAA officials estimate that it records more than 5,000 airline trades or leases per season, which are manually entered into its records. Furthermore, slot usage is often reported by the slot operator, but the slot holder is responsible for complying with the slot usage requirement. Therefore, FAA often has to analyze and correct differences in data submitted by a slot holder and the slot operator (i.e., the lessee).

FAA officials acknowledged some inaccuracies in their data and that their process is somewhat inefficient, but told us that they have identified instances when airlines have not met the 80 percent usage rate and required airlines to return the underutilized slots to FAA. In these cases, FAA has issued letters to airlines indicating that they had lost rights to their slot. Furthermore, FAA officials explained that they are replacing the existing software system, which they said will address some of the problems we identified in maintaining complete and accurate records and make their oversight of airlines' compliance with the usage requirement more efficient. In particular, the new system should reduce the amount of data that requires manual entry into their records system. FAA anticipates implementing the new system by the end of 2012. However, because the system is not yet operational and its design is not finalized, we do not know to what extent the new system will improve the accuracy of FAA's records or improve its ability to check airlines' compliance with the usage requirement.

FAA's administration of the slot rules provides airlines with large slot holdings an advantage over those airlines that hold few slots because they have more flexibility in meeting the 80 percent usage requirement. Specifically, FAA does not require that airlines report the same flight in a specific slot over the course of a reporting period, which essentially allows airlines that hold multiple slots within a slot period—30 minutes at the New York City airports and 1 hour at Reagan National—to apply the 80 percent usage requirement collectively to their pool of slots within that slot period, as opposed to each individual slot. For example, an airline that holds 5 slots within one slot period could hold but not operate one of its 5 slots (20 percent) and still meet the usage requirement if the other 4 were used at 100 percent by "rotating" 4 flights across its 5 allocated slots during the reporting period. FAA officials told us that they recognize that this method of applying the usage requirement provides more flexibility to airlines with multiple slots in a slot period, and that although this method is not specifically addressed in the slot control rules, it is not prohibited either. FAA officials told us that this method is a long-standing custom that has evolved within FAA over time. FAA has no written guidance for airlines describing the method. Most slot coordinators outside of the United States oversee compliance with the usage requirement based on each slot's individual usage. Port Authority officials said that measuring usage for each individual slot would reduce the incidence of airlines holding onto slots that they do not need, making some existing capacity available for redistribution. Representatives from four smaller slot-holding airlines told us they would favor FAA requiring airlines to apply the usage requirement to each individual slot, while representatives from five airlines—four of which have larger slot holdings—said they were opposed to it because it would reduce their scheduling flexibility. Using the current method for measuring usage of an airline's slot pool within a slot period, airlines have an additional incentive to obtain as many slots as possible to increase their operating flexibility without necessarily increasing their number of operations—which would be an inefficient use of limited airport capacity. Port Authority officials told us that airlines in the past have announced new air service without obtaining any new slots. However, the only way for an airline to add more flights without obtaining more slots is if that airline begins using a slot that it was not fully utilizing before. In addition, DOJ raised this as a concern in its comments on the US Airways and Delta Air Lines proposed slot swap, referring to the practice of airlines using flights on slots that exceed the 80 percent threshold to cover for an unused slot in the same slot period as "babysitting".[56]

Increasing the minimum usage requirement above 80 percent could also result in less capacity going unused. For example, according to Airports Council International in Europe, an airport organization that supports the European Commission proposal to increase the minimum usage requirement in Europe to 85 percent, increasing the slot usage requirement would encourage airlines to optimize their use of slots and allow slots that are not being used effectively to be returned and reallocated. Because airlines operating outside the United States generally schedule all of their slots, they tend to operate a higher percentage of their slots than in the United States. Even so, representatives from the Association of European Airlines told us that increasing the required usage rate could result in an unintended consequence of having airlines fly more aircraft than consumer demand requires on specific routes, and with lower load factors (percent of available seats filled with passengers), to meet the higher usage requirement. Although most U.S. airline representatives with whom we spoke said they opposed increasing the slot usage requirement, representatives from two airlines with small slot holdings said they would support increasing it and a representative from another airline supported increasing it if the new rate did not penalize for cancellations because of bad weather and other unforeseeable circumstances. Representatives at an airline with a large number of slots said that increasing the slot usage requirement above 80 percent would not increase efficiency because it would reduce airlines' flexibility to cope with unforeseeable events such as weather, air traffic control delays, or technical problems. On average, however, flight cancellations account for less than 2 percent of the total scheduled flights (the cancellation rates at the New York City area airports are generally higher than the system-wide average) and FAA may grant waivers to the minimum usage requirement under other unusual or unpredictable circumstances.[57]

Underutilized Capacity

Despite limits on airport capacity, flights operated at slot-controlled airports—as compared with flights at other like-sized airports that are not slot-controlled—

- tend to use smaller aircraft;
- are, in some instances, flown to the same destination at higher rates per day; and
- have lower overall load factors (percentage of available seats filled with passengers).

As a result, the level of passenger traffic at these airports is not as great as the number of slots could allow and would-be-new entrant airlines that could potentially offer lower fares or service to other destinations may be shut out of these markets. The potential inefficient use of slots by incumbent airlines at the New York City area airports as a way to block competitors' entry to the New York market has been examined before. Under FAA's 2006 proposed, but later withdrawn, congestion-management rule for LaGuardia, FAA proposed requiring airlines to use an average minimum aircraft size. FAA—in explaining its proposal— indicated that some inefficiencies at LaGuardia were related to airlines using smaller aircraft and that increasing the overall number of passengers without increasing the number of flights would result in a more efficient use of the national airspace system. Although FAA ultimately withdrew the proposed average minimum aircraft size requirement in 2008, the agency indicated that the concept behind the proposed minimum aircraft-size requirement remained valid because capacity cannot be considered merely on the basis of the number of aircraft being handled by FAA's Air Traffic Control system.[58] In particular, FAA cited certain market patterns involving multiple daily flights on small aircraft that were not related to the size of the community served, which indicated an inefficient use of slots or behavior that stifled competition. Similarly, in 2010, when DOJ commented on the competitive aspects of the proposed slot swap between Delta Air Lines and US

Airways at slot-controlled Reagan National and LaGuardia, it found that airlines engaged in what DOJ referred to as "slot hoarding" by flying excessive frequencies or using small planes.[59] While the use of smaller aircraft, high frequencies, and low load factors may be indications that airlines are hoarding slots as a way to keep competitors out of the slot-controlled airports, there are also possible market-based explanations for these tendencies. Without other evidence of airlines' motivations, all that can be determined is that flights at the slot controlled airports tend to use the available capacity more inefficiently than like-sized airports that are not slot-controlled. But, given that slots are a scarce resource and interest from new entrant airlines is known, this provides sufficient reason to improve slot utilization.

Aircraft Size

To examine the extent to which flights at slot-controlled airports use smaller aircraft (100 seats or fewer [60]), we conducted statistical analyses using data on aircraft size of scheduled passenger flights between domestic, large hub airports.[61] We analyzed airline schedule data that included, among other things, the scheduled flight date, origin and destination of the scheduled flight, and the size of the aircraft. We used data from one Thursday each in February 2011 and in August 2011.[62]

Thursdays are generally considered to be a high-demand day, and February and August are representative months for the winter and summer seasons, respectively.

Our analysis indicates that the proportion of flights using small aircraft is significantly greater at the slot-controlled airports than at other large hub airports that are not slot-controlled. The proportion of flights using small aircraft at slot-controlled airports ranged from 36 percent at LaGuardia to 25.8 percent at Newark, whereas the proportion of flights using small aircraft to and from large hub airports that are not slot-controlled was 16.4 percent. That is, the percent of flights using small aircraft at any of the slot-controlled airports was between 9.4 percent and 19.6 percent higher—depending on the airport—than the percent of flights using small aircraft at other non-slot-controlled large hub airports. We found that these differences were all statistically significant (see table 5). To some extent, the perimeter rules at Reagan National and LaGuardia contribute to the use of smaller aircraft at these airports because shorter haul flights are generally served by smaller aircraft, but also limit service to larger long-distance markets that use larger aircraft. Also, 11 out of the 60 hourly slots allowed under the High Density Rule slots at Reagan National are reserved for and require the use of smaller aircraft used for commuter flights. And, under LaGuardia's temporary order, FAA assigned some slots to airlines that held slot exemptions granted under AIR-21, which included slot exemptions for flights serving small communities using aircraft with fewer than 71 seats. See appendix V for a detailed discussion of our analysis and the results.

Table 5. Percentage Difference in Flights at Slot-Controlled Airports That Use Small Aircraft Compared with Flights at Non-Slot-Controlled Airports, 2011

Airport(s)	Percentage of flights that use small aircraft	Percentage differences in smallaircraft at slot-controlled airportscompared with other large hubairports that are not slot-controlled[a]
Newark	25.8 percent	9.4 percent more
JFK	26.6 percent	10.2 percent more
Reagan National	34.0 percent	17.6 percent more
LaGuardia	36.0 percent	19.6 percent more
All 4 U.S. slot-controlled airports	29.3 percent	12.9 percent more
All 3 New York City area slot-controlled airports	30.2 percent	13.8 percent more
Large hub airports that are not slot controlled	16.4 percent	N/A

Source: GAO analysis of airline schedule data.
N/A = not applicable.
[a]The percentage differences are all statistically significant.

To better understand the extent to which small aircraft are used at slot-controlled airports, we also developed a logistic regression model that controlled for other factors that are likely associated with aircraft size.[63] The model assessed whether scheduled passenger flights to or from slot-controlled airports tend to have a greater likelihood of being scheduled with small aircraft compared with flights to and from other large hub airports that are not slot-controlled. In addition, the model controlled for other factors that include (1) whether the origin or destination of the flight is a high-tourism airport,[64] (2) whether the airline marketing the flight is a "legacy" airline,[65] (3) the daily frequency of flights to the same destination by the same airline, and (4) the flight distance. Although the model controls for distance, which helps control the effect of the perimeter rules at Reagan National and LaGuardia, the model does not control for the designated commuter slots at Reagan National that are limited to commuter-sized aircraft.[66] However, FAA officials told us that based on their analysis, about 30 to 40 percent of slots that do not require the use of commuter aircraft also use commuter-sized aircraft. Also, as with any regression model, this analysis does not prove a causal relationship between different factors, such as slot control rules and an airlines' use of a small aircraft. Thus, the extent to which the slot-control rules, the perimeter rules at Reagan National and LaGuardia, and the commuter-slot designation at Reagan National contribute to underutilization at these airports is unknown. Other factors related to the use of small aircraft may not be fully controlled for, such as the type of passenger traffic. See appendix V for a detailed discussion of the model.

Table 6. Percentage Difference in Likelihood of a Flight's Using Small Aircraft at Slot-Controlled Airports Compared with Non-Slot-Controlled Airports

Slot-controlled airport(s)	Likelihood (as measured by odds ratio)[a] that a flight to or from a slot-controlledairport used a small aircraft compared withother large hub airports that are not slot-controlled
Newark	22 percent more likely[b]
JFK	63 percent more likely[c]
Reagan National	72 percent more likely[c]
LaGuardia	108 percent more likely[c]
All 4 U.S. slot-controlled airports	75 percent more likely[c]
All 3 New York City area slot-controlled airports	68 percent more likely[c]

Source: GAO analysis of airline schedule data.

Notes: The results of our analyses for 124 seat and 80 seat cutoffs also found odds ratio values greater than 1, and in some instances the results were more significant.

The percentage differences in the likelihood that a flight used a small aircraft presented here are based on odds ratios calculated from our model. Specifically, the likelihood equals the odds ratio minus 1, then multiplied by 100.

[a]See appendix V for a description of odds ratios. [b]Statistically significant at p-value <0.1.

[c]Statistically significant at p-value <0.01.

Similar to our analysis discussed above, the model results also suggest that airlines are more likely to use small aircraft for flights at slot-controlled airports than they are for flights at other large hub airports that are not slot-controlled. Specifically, when controlling for other factors that may be associated with using a small aircraft, flights to or from the four slot-controlled airports are between 22 percent and 108 percent more likely—depending on the airport—to use a small aircraft than flights that arrive and depart large hub airports that are not slot-controlled (see table 6). See appendix V for a detailed discussion of the model results.

According to representatives from some airlines with smaller slot holdings and some airport representatives, airlines with large slot portfolios have an incentive and the ability to fly smaller and more frequent flights at slot-controlled airports in a desire to hold on to slots they would otherwise not use because they do not want to lose them to a competitor. Of the 11 airlines that we interviewed for this review, representatives from 7 non-legacy airlines favored establishing minimum aircraft size requirements at the slot-controlled airports, while representatives from 3 legacy airlines opposed it.[67] Representatives from two airlines also said they would support a minimum aircraft size requirement if small aircraft could still be used to serve small communities. Representatives from two airlines who favored establishing a minimum aircraft size said that using small aircraft between major markets is a particularly inappropriate use of constrained airspace. However, representatives from legacy airlines that we spoke with said establishing minimum aircraft size requirements would negatively affect service to small- and medium-sized markets and that it would limit their ability to use aircraft sizes that are most appropriate to meet customer needs, for example, regarding schedule frequency and market conditions.

Flight Frequency

In analyzing airline schedule data, we found instances when airlines scheduled flights to or from slot-controlled airports for the same destination at a more frequent rate than other large hub airports that are not slot-controlled. For example, airlines might fly smaller aircraft at higher rates to provide frequent shuttle service for business travelers. We found, however, that on February 11, 2011, one airline scheduled more than 20 daily flights from LaGuardia to Philadelphia—a distance of 96 miles by air—and that some of those flights were scheduled 10 minutes or less apart. As of June 21, 2012, the airline had reduced the number of daily nonstop flights on this route to 15. Representatives from the airline operating these flights said the high frequency of flights between LaGuardia to Philadelphia is driven by consumer demand and provides more choice for customers. They also said that almost all of the passengers on these flights are connecting to other flights and that the airline is not competing with other airlines in this market, but with cars and trains. To better understand the extent to which airlines schedule flights to or from slot-controlled airports for the same destination at short intervals, we examined the frequency of scheduled flights to the same destination by the same airline between all large hub airports for one day in February 2011.[68] February is a low demand month in which airlines at slot-controlled airports might not reduce the number of scheduled flights as they might at other airports that are not slot-controlled. Rather, the airline might operate smaller, more frequent flights to meet the 80 percent usage requirement.[69] Our analysis found that of the scheduled flights to or from the same destination by the same airline within 15 minutes of one another, LaGuardia accounted for 17 of the 50 total scheduled flights identified (34 percent). The airport with the next highest proportion was Philadelphia International with 11 of the 50 identified flights (22 percent) – all of which were scheduled to fly to or from LaGuardia. Moreover, the 11 scheduled flights that we identified within 15 minutes of one another operated by the same airline between LaGuardia and Philadelphia had an average aircraft size of 38 seats. When we examined scheduled flights within 30 minutes of one another to or from the same destination by the same airline, LaGuardia still had the highest share with 70 of the 264 identified flights (27 percent), followed by Philadelphia International with a share of 29 of the 264 identified flights (see fig. 4). While current slot control rules do not prohibit airlines from this type of scheduling practice, FAA officials noted that the slot swap between Delta Air Lines and US Airways have enabled these airlines to use their resources more efficiently. Port Authority officials told us that they believe that any airline that schedules a second flight to the same destination within a slot period (30 minutes at the New York City area airports) should have to demonstrate that there is demand for that second flight that could not be met by a single larger aircraft.

Load Factors

We also examined FAA data on average load factors (percentage of seats occupied) at large hub airports for all domestic scheduled passenger flights in calendar year 2011 and found that flights at slot-controlled airports were overall less full than flights at other large hub airports that are not slot-controlled. As shown in figure 5, we found that Reagan National (70 percent) and LaGuardia (72 percent) had the lowest average load factors for 2011 among the large hub airports, with Newark (77 percent) tied with Boston Logan International and Philadelphia International for the third lowest load factor.

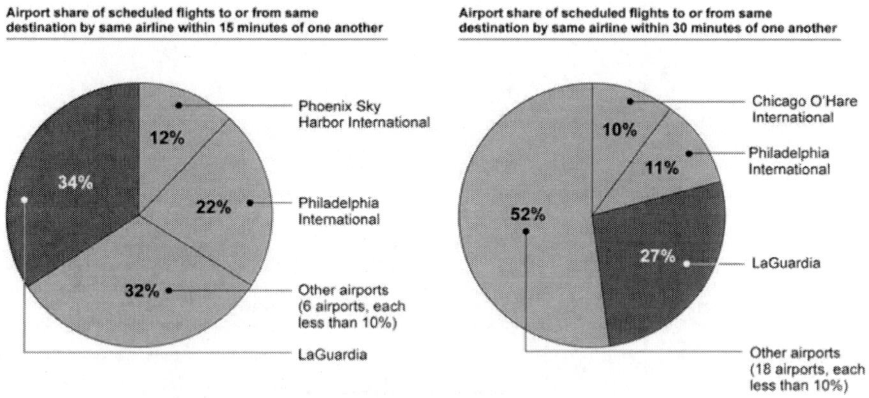

Source: GAO analysis of airlane schedule data.

Notes: "Other" airports in the 15 minute chart include Charlotte/Douglas International, Chicago O'Hare International, Dallas-Fort Worth International, Las Vegas McCarran International, Newark, and San Diego International.

"Other" airports in the 30 minute chart include Hartsfield-Jackson Atlanta International, Boston Logan International, BWI, Charlotte/Douglas International, Dallas-Fort Worth International, Denver International, Detroit Metro Wayne County, Dulles, Las Vegas McCarran International, Los Angeles International, Orlando International, Miami International, Newark, Phoenix Sky Harbor International, Reagan National, San Diego International, San Francisco International, and Tampa International.

Figure 4. Airports' Share of Scheduled Flights to or from the Same Destination by the Same Airline within 15 Minutes or 30 Minutes of One Another, February 2011.

According to Port Authority officials and some airline representatives, some airlines at slot-controlled airports might operate flights with lower load factors to help meet the 80 percent usage requirement and maintain control of their slots, whereas flights with similarly low load factors at a non-slot-controlled airport might be discontinued. However, another factor to explain the comparatively low load factors at New York airports is the relatively high airline yields (a measurement of airline revenue per mile). Yields at Newark, LaGuardia, and Reagan National are some of the highest among the large hub airports, which means that a flight with a low load factor may still be profitable for these airlines. If the objective is to maximize the number of passengers at these airports, however, this represents an inefficient use of airport capacity.

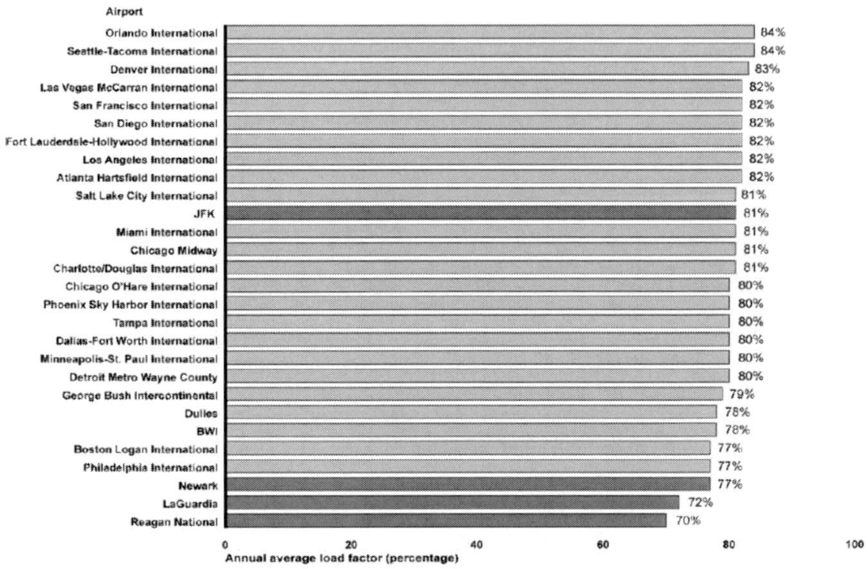

Source: GAO analysis of DOT data.

Figure 5. Average Load Factors at Large Hub Airports for Scheduled Flights during 2011.

Slot Control Rules Limit New Entry and Hinder Competition

Representatives from low cost and other airlines that have sought to obtain slots told us that they have had difficulty gaining access to slot-controlled airports. Airline representatives seeking slots at these airports told us that they have spoken to FAA, but generally not enough slots are available or the slots are at undesirable times of day (e.g., early morning or late evening) for these airlines to operate profitable service.[70] DOT officials are also aware of the access issue, and it was a focus of the previous congestion-management rulemakings and an advisory Aviation Rulemaking Committee report for the New York City area airports.[71] DOT also took steps to mitigate potential competitive harm from the Delta Air Lines and US Airways proposed slot swap by requiring divestiture of some slots at the airports to airlines with small or no presence at the airports. DOJ, in commenting on competition at

LaGuardia and Reagan National during the Delta Air Lines and US Airways proposed slot swap in 2010, indicated that the lack of availability of slots is a substantial barrier to entry at those airports, especially for low cost airlines. Based on literature that we reviewed, airfares can drop up to 30 percent on a flight route as a result of a low cost airline entering the airport and beginning service on that route.[72] Because average airfares at the slot-controlled airports are some of the highest among domestic large hub airports, the entrance of low cost competition could be helpful in bringing down airfares at those airports. While in some cases Congress has directed that new airport capacity in the form of slot exemptions be allocated to new entrants or "limited incumbents," which are generally low cost airlines, those new slot exemptions are a small percentage of the total slots at the airport. Figure 6 shows that the proportion of passenger traffic handled by the nonlegacy airlines in 2011 generally is smaller at slot-controlled airports compared with the other 24 large hub airports.

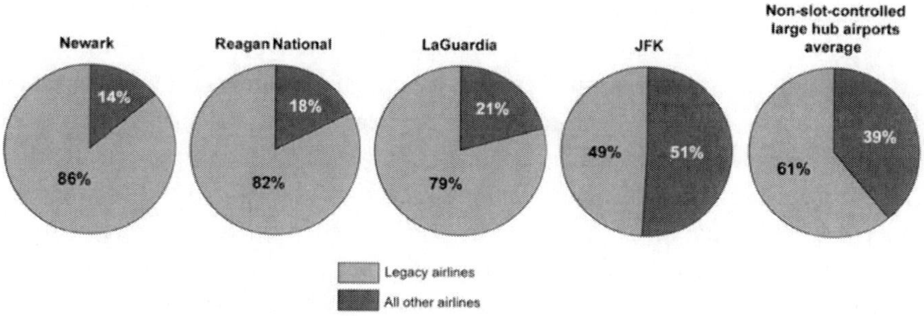

Source: GAO analysis of DOT data.

Figure 6. Proportion of Legacy and Other Airline Passenger Traffic at Slot-Controlled and Non-Slot-Controlled Large Hub Airports, 2011.

DOJ also indicated in 2010 that increasing the number of slots held by two large legacy carriers at the slot-controlled LaGuardia and Reagan National airports would make it more difficult for new entrants to obtain slots because large legacy carriers would have greater incentives to forestall entry by refusing to sell or lease their slots. Representatives of some airlines with few slot-holdings told us that they believe that the airlines that hold the majority of slots at the airports are hesitant or unwilling to lease to them. In general, airlines holding a slot under FAA's slot rules may lease or trade slots to other airlines and can select which airlines they lease or trade slots with.[73] Airlines may have legitimate business reasons for leasing slots to code-share partners, for example, to feed into the lessor airlines' network. In addition, representatives from large slot-holding airlines said that they may hold onto slots that they do not currently need by leasing to other airlines in case they want them back later. In general, airlines only return slots to FAA that airlines are unable to find other airlines interested in leasing or buying. Airlines with large slot holdings also noted that they have made substantial financial investments in terminal facilities, such as terminals at JFK, at the slot-controlled airports. While the slots that are returned can be reallocated to other airlines, including new entrants or limited incumbents, the returned slots generally are the least desirable—such as early morning or late evening or weekend-only—and may only be for a couple of months, which makes them undesirable for airlines trying to build year-round service.

According to Port Authority officials and some airline representatives, if FAA were to limit the length of time that an airline could hold on to a slot when that airline was not using or leasing it to another airline—after which the slots would be withdrawn by FAA for reallocation—this could provide opportunities for new entrants or small slot-holders to obtain slots. Representatives from most of the airlines we contacted, except the legacy airlines, said they favored limiting how long airlines can hold onto slots they are not using. However, representatives from a legacy airline said that imposing such a holding limit is unnecessary because slots do not go unused. These representatives told us that although there are some instances that on paper it appears that airlines are not using their slots, the airlines are actually holding the slots by leasing them to other airlines for a future time when they want to use them again. Also, the representatives noted that airlines may be holding onto slots for long periods of time (e.g., over multiple seasons) because the temporary slot orders for the New York City area airports do not allow airlines to buy or sell slots.

FAA's administration of its slot rules can hinder the ability of airlines to add service at slot-controlled airports because it does not provide complete transparency about what slots are available. FAA officials said that, upon request, FAA provides airlines with lists of slot holders and operators as well as available slots, but some airline representatives and Port Authority officials told us that the format of this information does not make clear what slots are available. Furthermore, as discussed earlier, because of discrepancies in FAA's slot allocation records, it is unclear whether the information provided to airlines is accurate. Port Authority officials recommend public reporting of slot leasing and slot usage, including the reasons why the slots are not being operated (e.g., flights were not scheduled or were cancelled) to provide transparency of information. In addition, although FAA requires the submission of certain records of all trades and leases between airlines, it does not require the submission of the information—such as the origin and destination that a lessee intends to use for the slot—that would allow FAA or DOT to monitor the extent to which leases occur between nonpartner airlines.[74] While DOT officials questioned the efficacy of reviewing data currently collected on airline slot leases in isolation, additional information relating to the transaction could be helpful. But, officials noted that even with additional data, the department faces a very high burden of proof in alleging that an airline is engaged in unfair or deceptive competitive practices.[75] DOT officials told us that they believe that under the current temporary orders, they are unable to react to certain market failures at slot-controlled airports, such as inefficient use of constrained airspace. DOT officials could not comment further on this because of the pending Slot Management and Transparency rulemaking for the New York City area airports. DOJ officials told us that, unless they have an open investigation, they do not monitor ongoing day-to-day activities such as short-term leases at slot-controlled airports. An investigation of competition-related issues at these airports is generally "triggered" by a transaction such as an airline merger or slot swap, although DOJ may also investigate in response to complaints, such as complaints by airlines unable to obtain slots. Additional information on leases and trades of slots, particularly the relationship between the lessor and the lessee, would allow FAA to provide more complete information to airlines on the availability of slots, which increases transparency.

CONCLUSION

Because the New York City airports are both capacity constrained and among the nation's most sought after by airlines to serve, FAA has had to institute slot controls to manage congestion and resultant delays. It is therefore important that slots allocated to airlines are efficiently utilized, thereby maximizing the airports' available capacity, or reallocated to other airlines that will use them efficiently, which could, in turn, provide access to new entrant airlines that offer new service destinations and lower fares. Despite these goals, we found that considerable existing capacity is not being used or is used inefficiently at these airports. Certain aspects of the slot control rules, as well as FAA's administration of them, contribute to this situation and, thus, may hinder the ability of some new entrant airlines to obtain slots at the four U.S.

slot-controlled airports. In particular, although the current slot control rules require slot holders to operate their slots 80 percent of the time, they do not require slot holders to schedule a flight for each of their slots. And, as opposed to airlines operating at slot-controlled airports outside the United States that generally schedule flights for all of their slots, domestic airlines operating at the U.S. slot-controlled airports do not always schedule all of their slots, which contributes to capacity going unused. Further, FAA's current recordkeeping and process for reviewing airline slot usage data do not provide sufficient assurance that it can adequately identify when airlines do not meet the 80 percent usage requirement. Not requiring airlines to report usage data in a standard format or having management systems that can adequately compile data received in different formats, as well as its reliance on airlines' self-reported data and discrepancies in its slot allocation record, hinders FAA's ability to check compliance with the slot usage requirement. Moreover, because FAA does not calculate the actual slot usage rates for airlines, the amount of capacity that goes unused is unknown, which limits FAA's ability to manage slots or set policy for the airspace. FAA's planned upgrades to its slot management software later this year will hopefully improve its oversight capabilities, but not without better and more standardized reporting by airlines. Other practices that affect utilization, however, will not be fixed with the new software. For example, FAA allows an airline to apply the usage requirement across its entire pool of slots within a slot time period, rather than applying the requirement to its individual slot—a practice that provides advantages to airlines with large slot holdings over those with small slot holdings in meeting the requirement. This practice can lead to underutilization of individual slots and hinder other airlines' ability to obtain slots at these airports. Limitations in FAA's recordkeeping, particularly the discrepancies in its slot allocation records, as well as its lack of information on the relationship between slot lessors and lessees and public disclosure on the availability of slots and lease information, also hinder access to new entrant airlines at slot-controlled airports.

RECOMMENDATIONS FOR EXECUTIVE ACTION

To help maximize the use of available capacity at slot-controlled airports, enhance competition through greater airline access to slots, and enhance transparency of slot information, we recommend that the Secretary of

Transportation direct the FAA Administrator to take the following five actions:

- require airlines to report usage data in a standard format at the end of each reporting period or ensure that future slot management systems have the capability to compile data in different formats;
- periodically calculate the rates at which airlines are scheduling and using their slots;
- apply slot rules to individual slots, as opposed to pools of slots within a slot period;
- periodically disclose information, which may include current slot holders and operators, on currently available slots; and
- collect and disclose data, including the relationship between lessors and lessees, on slot leases.

Furthermore, with respect to possible future regulatory action, we recommend that DOT Secretary consider requiring airlines to schedule a certain percentage, or all, of their slot allocations, similar to practices maintained elsewhere in the world.

AGENCY COMMENTS AND OUR EVALUATION

We provided DOT, MWAA, the Port Authority of New York and New Jersey, DOJ, and the Department of Homeland Security (DHS) with a draft of this report for their review and comment. DOT's Office of the Secretary and FAA provided technical comments that we incorporated as appropriate. In addition, in comments e-mailed to us, FAA reiterated that the slot control rules at the three New York City area airports and Reagan National were adopted primarily to manage congestion and delay at these airports by limiting planned operations during peak hours. Officials highlighted that complex issues arise with the allocation and use of a scarce resource like airport slots and that congestion-management policy objectives must be balanced with realistic competition and market access goals. FAA indicated that economic and compliance benefits and costs to stakeholders and regulatory and statutory guidelines must also be considered. We agree that the slot control rules can manage congestion and delay and that issues may arise when allocating a scarce resource. We also believe that the rules can be improved to make the use of current capacity more efficient, as well as enhance competition.

Officials also noted that DOT's Office of the Secretary and FAA are developing rules to replace the temporary slot control Orders at the New York City area airports with more permanent rules. As stated in our report, these temporary rules have been extended twice, creating a level of uncertainty in the market about when the final rule will be issued and what it will contain. While we acknowledge DOT's and FAA's efforts to develop a permanent rule, we also believe that FAA could take separate action now to help maximize the use of available capacity at slot-controlled airports, enhance competition through greater airline access to slots, and enhance transparency of slot information.

MWAA agreed with our recommendations to improve FAA's oversight of slot utilization and encouraged DOT to adopt these recommendations to better manage available airport capacity and provide a more transparent process. However, MWAA disagreed with our conclusion that the additional beyond-perimeter slot exemptions at Reagan National are likely to have a limited effect on the Washington, D.C., area airports and can be supported by terminal capacity at Reagan National. In the comments, MWAA indicated that the impact of the beyond-perimeter flights should be viewed in the broader context of other changes under way at Reagan National, for example, those resulting from legacy carrier mergers, the Delta Air Lines and US Airways slot-swap transaction, and other recent commercial slot transactions. MWAA believes that these factors are changing the operating character of Reagan National, change that may require considerable additional capital investment for extensive facility modifications. However, our review was expressly limited to the impact of the additional slot exemptions authorized in 2012, and not the cumulative effect of previously authorized beyond-perimeter slot exemptions and other slot-related and commercial changes. The report includes the views of MWAA management with regard to the specific challenges faced by the expansion of beyond-perimeter slot exemptions throughout, but our overall assessment remains that the effect of the 2012 FAA Reauthorization slot exemptions is manageable and that the impact on other Washington, D.C., area airports is relatively small. On this point, MWAA disagrees with our report in regard to the financial impact of potential passenger erosion on Dulles International. Our report does recognize the potential effect on per-passenger airline costs at Dulles and Reagan National, but also states that this estimated effect is a worst case scenario and should be considered in light of (1) the recent substantial increases in costs from capital investments at Dulles that are unrelated to the new slot exemptions; (2) the passenger growth forecast by FAA that could ameliorate that erosion; (3) the views of airlines and credit-rating agencies that airline service is also dependent on market demand, which is strong in this region; and (4) the "extraordinary coverage protection payments" provision in the airline lease agreements that may allow MWAA to share debt service between the two airports should they need to and the possibility of revising this provision in the new lease. Finally, as we indicate in the report, we concur with MWAA that because some of the new beyond-perimeter flights only started in August 2012, the actual impact of the new beyond-perimeter flights cannot yet be fully determined. MWAA also provided some specific updated information, which we incorporated as appropriate in the report.

The Port Authority of New York and New Jersey provided written comments, agreeing with the report's conclusions and recommendations. The Port Authority of New York and New Jersey provided some clarifications that we incorporated as appropriate. DHS, on behalf of TSA, also provide some clarifications that we incorporated. DOJ provided no comments.

Susan A. Fleming
Director,
Physical Infrastructure Issues

APPENDIX I: OBJECTIVES, SCOPE, AND METHODOLOGY

In this report, we reviewed (1) the potential effects of increasing the number of beyond-perimeter slot exemptions at Reagan National and (2) whether slot control rules at the four U.S. slot-controlled airports are working to reduce congestion, while maximizing available capacity and encouraging competition.

To review the potential effects of increasing the number of beyond-perimeter slot exemptions at Reagan National, we

- compared airside capacity assessments with actual usage;
- reviewed terminal space needs;
- assessed the impact on the additional beyond-perimeter flights on passenger traffic, capital financing, security screening wait times, and noise; and
- interviewed officials from the Federal Aviation Administration (FAA), the Metropolitan Washington Airports Authority (MWAA),

and the Baltimore-Washington International Thurgood Marshall Airport (BWI), as well as representatives from airlines[1] and others.

Regarding airside capacity, we analyzed data on the volume of aircraft operations at Reagan National, regulations and FAA actions regarding slot allocations at the airport, and a capacity assessment conducted by an FAA contractor. With respect to terminal capacity, we observed the airport's baggage handling equipment, gates, ticket counter space, and security screening facilities; reviewed usage data on gates and parking lots; and discussed plans to expand terminal and security screening space with MWAA officials.

To assess the maximum impact that the new beyond-perimeter flights would have on passenger traffic, we assumed that the new flights would be 100-percent full and that all passengers would be shifting from Dulles to Reagan National. This provided the highest possible estimate of the loss of passengers and the associated rise in cost per enplaned passenger at Dulles because of the new beyond-perimeter flights at Reagan National. However, for a variety of reasons, it is unlikely that the number of passengers shifting from Dulles to Reagan National would actually be this high. First, the new flights are unlikely to draw travelers solely from Dulles. For example, consumers who have a strong preference for flying out of Reagan National might have been choosing to fly from Reagan on a connecting basis but will now have a direct choice and, despite the likelihood of a substantially higher fare, some of these passengers will opt for the more expensive direct flight. Similarly, some travelers might shift to the new flights at Reagan National from BWI. Second, the availability of the new flights may induce some pricing impacts that could influence travelers' decisions. For example, airlines that fly the same routes from Dulles may attempt to maintain their traffic by lowering prices on those routes to better compete for passengers who now have a nonstop choice from Reagan National. This would likely mitigate the flow of passengers from Dulles to Reagan National, and may even induce some new travelers on these routes. And finally, although the new routes will likely be very popular, it is possible that not all seats will be sold indicating that not all seats are filled with passengers who would have previously chosen Dulles. For these various reasons, it is likely that our "worst case" estimate of the number of passengers shifting from Dulles to Reagan National is likely overstated. We did not include the within-perimeter flights that were converted to beyond-perimeter slot exemptions in our analysis because there were too many unknown factors, such as whether the passengers those flights were connecting or originating at Reagan National and the load factors on those flights.

Regarding the new beyond-perimeter flights' impact on capacity financing, using our estimate of the number of passengers who could shift from using Dulles to Reagan National, we asked MWAA to estimate the impact on the cost per enplaned passenger at the two airports. We also discussed the methodology that MWAA used and determined that its methods were sufficiently reliable for our purposes. We also reviewed credit-rating reports on MWAA and discussed the reports with rating agency officials. Moreover, we reviewed passenger traffic and airfare and Dulles and BWI data relating to the beyond-perimeter flight destinations that were added between 2000 and 2004.

With respect to the impact that the new beyond-perimeter flights could have on aircraft noise, we reviewed the most recent noise compatibility report on Reagan National and noise complaints since 2008 and interviewed individuals from community groups concerned about aircraft noise at Reagan National as well as officials from the Washington Council of Governments, the Arlington County (Va.) Council, MWAA, and FAA.

To assess the impact that the new beyond-perimeter flights could have on passenger security screening wait times, we asked the Transportation Security Administration (TSA) to estimate, using its security screening throughput model, how the wait time would be affected. As inputs to the model, we provided TSA with the flight times for the new beyond-perimeter flights, data on the maximum number of passengers on those flights, and the screening checkpoints that the passengers would use. We did not report the precise estimates of wait time changes because they would imply a greater level of precision than the model could reasonably provide.

To review whether slot controls at U.S. slot-controlled airports are working to reduce congestion, while maximizing available capacity and encouraging competition, we analyzed airline schedule data and FAA slot allocation data to determine the rate at which slots at slot-controlled airports are scheduled. We also analyzed and compared and contrasted airline schedule data on aircraft size and flight frequency and Department of Transportation (DOT) data on average annual load factors and passenger traffic at the four slot-controlled airports with the remaining large hub airports[2] that are not slot-controlled. We interviewed officials from DOT; FAA; Department of Justice (DOJ); MWAA; and the Port Authority of New York and New Jersey, and interviewed representatives from 11 airlines that currently serve or have interest in serving one or more U.S. slot-controlled airport. We also contacted other stakeholders, including representatives from Airlines For America; the International Air Transport Association; Airports Council International, North America; and others, about slot control issues. We also reviewed slot control regulations for the four U.S. slot-controlled airports and obtained and analyzed applicable federal laws, regulations, and agency orders. In addition, we reviewed studies on airline competition, airport capacity, and demand management measures, including slot controls, as well as the slot reform proposal for the European Union and the Worldwide Slot Guidelines.

To calculate the rate at which slot allocations for scheduled passenger flights are scheduled at slot-controlled airports, we divided the total daily scheduled passenger flights within slot-controlled hours for a specific day and airport by the total number of daily slot allocations (provided by FAA) for that day and airport. We obtained airline schedule data from Innovata for scheduled passenger flights for the third week of February and August 2011 for JFK, Newark, LaGuardia, and Reagan National. FAA provided the daily total slot allocation numbers for scheduled passenger flights during slot-controlled hours for the same days for JFK, Newark, LaGuardia, and Reagan National.[3] FAA officials told us that the third week of the month is most representative of the month. To further examine schedule rates at Newark, we also obtained and analyzed daily slot allocations and airline schedule data for the third Saturday of April, May, June, July, September, and October 2011 for Newark. During our review FAA reported discrepancies in the slot allocation numbers provided to us. Specifically, FAA does not systematically update their slot allocation records with the lists of returned slots received from airlines each season for JFK and Newark. As a result, the data on slot allocations used for our analysis for JFK and Newark generally represents the number of flights initially allocated to each airline for the season rather than the final number they held.

To examine whether flights at slot-controlled airports use smaller aircraft, we conducted statistical analyses, including the construction of a logistic regression model to assess whether flights at slot-controlled airports use smaller aircraft than flights at other large hub airports that are not slot-controlled, while controlling for other factors that are likely associated with aircraft size, such as the flight distance (see app. V for more details on our model and results). We analyzed Innovata airline schedule data for one Thursday each in February 2011 and in August 2011.[4] Thursdays are generally considered to be a high-demand day, and February and August are representative months for the winter and summer seasons, respectively. We calculated the proportion of scheduled passenger flights arriving or departing each large hub airport that use aircraft with 100 seats or fewer. We also compared and contrasted the proportion of flights using aircraft with 100 seats or fewer departing or arriving slot-controlled airports with other large hub airports that are not slot-controlled. We tested that the difference was statistically significant. Since a variety of factors, in addition to slot controls, may be correlated with the use of a small aircraft, we developed a logistic regression model. The model assessed whether flights to or from slot-controlled airports used an aircraft with 100 seats or fewer compared with flights that arrive and depart other large hub airports that are not slot-controlled, while controlling for other factors that include (1) whether the origin or destination of the flight is a high-tourism airport,[5] (2) whether the airline marketing the flight is a legacy airline,[6] (3) the daily frequency of flights to the same destination by the same airline, and (4) the flight distance. We also conducted alternative scenarios examining aircraft with 124 seats or fewer (the median-sized aircraft in our sample) and 80 seats or fewer. See appendix V for more details on the logistic regression model and results.

To examine closely-scheduled flights to the same destination by the same airline, we analyzed airline schedule data, obtained from Innovata, for all flights arriving or departing FAA-identified large hub airports on Thursday February 10, 2011. For this analysis we calculated the number of minutes between each flight and the flight immediately prior to and following on the same route and by the same airline. We then identified those flights with another flight less than or equal to15 or 30 minutes apart, and calculated the proportion of such flights from each airport.

Average annual load factor data and average annual airline yield data for large hub airports was obtained from DOT's T-100 database, which includes operational data collected from airlines and DOT's origin and destination survey, respectively. To calculate airlines' proportion of passenger traffic on domestic scheduled passenger flights, we obtained and analyzed data from DOT's origin and destination survey for 2011 at each of the large hub airports.

To assess the reliability of airline schedule data, and DOT's T-100 and origin and destination survey, we (1) reviewed existing documentation related to the data sources and (2) interviewed knowledgeable agency officials and representatives about the data. We determined that the data were sufficiently reliable for the purposes of this review.

Appendix II: Comparative Information on Major Airports in the New York City and Washington, D.C., Area

Airport	JFK	LaGuardia	Newark	Reagan National	Dulles	BWI
Location	Queens County, NY, 15 miles from midtown Manhattan	Borough of Queens, New York City, 8 miles from midtown Manhattan	Newark and Elizabeth, NJ, 14 miles from Manhattan	Arlington County, VA, 3 miles from downtown Washington, D.C.	Chantilly, VA, 26 miles from downtown Washington, D.C.	Anne Arundel County, MD, 10 miles south of Baltimore and 32miles north of Washington, D.C.
Operator	Port Authority of New York and New Jersey	Port Authority of New York and New Jersey	Port Authority of New York and New Jersey	Metropolitan Washington Airports Authority	Metropolitan Washington Airports Authority	Maryland Department of Transportation's Aviation Administration
Acres of land	4,930	680	2,027	733	11,830	3,596
Number of runways	4 14,572 feet 11,351 feet 10,000 feet 8,400 feet	2 both are 7,000 feet	3 11,000 feet 9,980 feet 6,800 feet	3 6,869 feet 5,204 feet 4,911 feet	4 2 are 11,500 feet 10,500 feet 9,400 feet	4 10,502 feet 9,501 feet 6,000 feet 5,000 feet
Number of gates[a]	124	76	115	44	139	68
Number of airlines[a]	77	17	28	11	29	11
Airline holding the most slots[b]	Delta Air Lines (33 percent)	Delta Air Lines (44 percent)	United Airlines (75 percent)	US Airways (54 percent)	United Airlines (73 percent)c	Southwest Airlines (57 percent)[c]
2010 enplanements	22,892,372	11,988,578	16,542,619	8,726,183	11,251,041	10,770,973
2011 enplanements	23,585,722	11,983,322	16,786,357	9,039,072	11,020,479	10,985,559

Airport	JFK	LaGuardia	Newark	Reagan National	Dulles	BWI
Change in enplanements from 2010 to 2011	3 percent	0 percent	1.5 percent	3.6 percent	(2 percent)	2 percent
Domestic share of 2011 enplanements	50 percent	96 percent	66 percent	98 percent	72 percent	98 percent

Sources: MWAA, Port Authority of New York and New Jersey, BWI, and BTS.

[a]As of June 2012.

[b]As of May 15, 2012.

[c]Because Dulles and BWI are not slot-controlled airports, the data reflect the airlines' percentage of total scheduled departures on May 15, 2012, rather than the percentage of slots held.

APPENDIX III: HISTORY OF SLOT CONTROL RULES AND RELATED ACTIONS

Slot controls at Reagan National and the New York City area airports were first implemented in the late 1960s. Since then, the number of takeoffs and landings permitted at these airports has been revised periodically as well as the slot control procedures that airlines should follow. In addition, since the 1950s at LaGuardia and since the 1960s at Reagan National, airlines have been subject to limitations on the distance of their nonstop flights known as "perimeter rules." Figure 7 shows when major events related to slot controls and perimeter rules occurred at the four airports.

Date	Reagan National	JFK	LaGuardia	Newark
April 1969	High Density Rule implemented	High Density Rule implemented	High Density Rule implemented	High Density Rule implemented
October 1970				High Density Rule suspended
December 1981	1,000-mile limit for nonstop flights set			
October 1985	1,250-mile limit for nonstop flights enacted			
April 2000	Twelve beyond-perimeter slot exemptions authorized	High Density Rule to be phased out by January 1, 2007	High Density Rule to be phased out by January 1, 2007	
December 2003	Twelve more beyond-perimeter slot exemptions authorized			
August 2006			Congestion management rule proposed	
January 2007		High Density Rule expired	High Density Rule expired Temporary controls implemented by FAA order	
March 2008		Temporary controls implemented by FAA order		
April 2008			Congestion management rule proposed (second round)	
May 2008		Congestion management rule proposed		Congestion management rule proposed
June 2008				Temporary controls implemented by FAA order
October 2008		Congestion management rule effective December 2008	Congestion management rule effective December 2008	Congestion management rule effective December 2008
October 2009		Congestion management rule rescinded	Congestion management rule rescinded	Congestion management rule rescinded
April 2011		Temporary slot controls extended until a congestion management rule is effective or October 2013	Temporary slot controls extended until a congestion management rule is effective or October 2013	Temporary slot controls extended until a congestion management rule is effective or October 2013
October 2011	Slots transfer between Delta Air Lines and US Airways at Reagan National and LaGuardia approved, with conditions (final application)		Slots transfer between Delta Air Lines and US Airways at Reagan National and LaGuardia approved, with conditions (final application)	
February 2012	Eight more beyond-perimeter slot exemptions authorized and eight within-perimeter slots authorized to be converted to beyond perimeter slot exemptions			
May 2012	Eight new beyond-perimeter slot exemptions awarded to airlines			

DOT Office of the Secretary/FAA action

Congressional action

Source: GAO analysis of U.S. Code and FAA orders.

Figure 7. Timeline of Major Actions Taken Regarding Slot Controls and Perimeter Rules at the Major New York City Area Airports and Reagan National.

Slot controls were implemented in 1969 when the Federal Aviation Administration (FAA) designated JFK, LaGuardia, Newark, Chicago O'Hare, and Washington National[1] as high density airports. In implementing what became known as the High Density Rule, FAA indicated that slot controls were needed to provide relief from excessive delays at these airports.[2] Under the rule, FAA required airlines to obtain slots to operate during certain hours at those airports and initially imposed limits of 60 takeoffs and landings per hour at Newark, LaGuardia, and Washington National, and 80 per hour at JFK. In 1970, FAA lifted the High Density Rule at Newark because of a lower level of usage of the slots at that airport as evidenced by, among other things, that the average number of aircraft operations at peak hours was 18 less than the 60 slots allowed.[3] In general, Newark was not slot-controlled from late October 1970 until 2008.[4] FAA implemented the High Density Rule in 1969 and, because of its effectiveness in reducing congestion and delays, extended it for an indefinite period of time in 1973. Airline scheduling committees, operating under then-authorized antitrust immunity, conferred by the Civil Aeronautics Board, initially allocated the slots. However, according to FAA officials, after the Airline Deregulation Act of 1978 was enacted into law,[5] increased airline competition made it more difficult for the scheduling committees to agree on slot allocations and antitrust immunity for the committees' operations expired under the terms of the Airline Deregulation Act. In 1986, as a part of its High Density Rule, FAA replaced the scheduling committees with slot procedures such as providing for the withdrawal of slots not used at least 65 percent of the time, the voluntary return of slots, the reallocation of withdrawn and returned slots, and allowing airlines to buy, sell, or lease their slots.[6] In implementing this 1986 minimum slot usage rule, FAA cited the Department of Justice's (DOJ) concerns that a use or lose provision "may be necessary to prevent large carriers or several large carriers from hoarding slots in an attempt to restrict service to drive up fares or keep smaller competitors from entering into or expanding in certain markets."

In the 1990s, we,[7] Transportation Research Board,[8] Department of Transportation (DOT)[9], and new entrant carriers, respectively, studied the High Density Rule and presented reports and congressional testimony that the High Density Rule was a barrier to competition and to improved service, in part because new airlines were unable to establish service at the slot-controlled airports because of the lack of slot availability.[10] Subsequently, in April 2000, Congress required that the application of the High Density Rule be phased out at JFK and LaGuardia airports by January 1, 2007, and directed DOT, in the interim to grant exemptions to the High Density Rule to allow for a certain number of flights operated by new entrant airlines and flights serving small hub and nonhub airports if the aircraft had fewer than 71 seats.[11] By the fall of 2000, DOT had granted the exemptions required by statute, and airlines had added 300 scheduled flights at LaGuardia, resulting in a 144 percent increase in the average minutes of delay for arriving flights, from 15.52 minutes in March 2000 (a month before the law was enacted) to 37.86 minutes in September 2000. Furthermore, FAA reported that by September 2000, flight delays at LaGuardia accounted for 25 percent of the nation's delays, compared with 10 percent during the previous year. To address congestion at LaGuardia, FAA reduced the number of daily slot exemptions and distributed the exemptions through a lottery.[12]

In 2006, FAA proposed a congestion management rule for LaGuardia that would have replaced the High Density Rule when it expired on January 1, 2007.[13] The proposed rule would have encouraged the use of larger aircraft by implementing an average aircraft size requirement (with proposed exemptions for service to small communities). However, because FAA did not expect to complete the congestion management rule before the High Density Rule expired, the agency imposed temporary slot controls at LaGuardia effective on January 1, 2007 (a maximum of 75 slots per hour) and required airlines to use slots at least 80 percent of the time.[14] In addition, in 2007, the New York Aviation Rulemaking Committee[15] explored ways to reduce congestion and efficiently allocate scare capacity at the New York City area airports, including making operational and infrastructure improvements; using congestion pricing or auctions; requiring airlines to use larger aircraft; modifying gate allocations; amending or eliminating the perimeter rule; implementing priority aviation traffic preferences; or following International Air Transport Association's Worldwide Slot Guidelines.

After JFK and Newark airports experienced flight delays during the summer of 2007, in October 2007, FAA announced operational targets of 81 flights per hour from 3:00 p.m. to 7:59 p.m. at JFK. In March 2008, by order, FAA imposed temporary slot controls at JFK (a maximum of 81 slots per hour) [16] and in June 2008, by order, imposed temporary slot controls at Newark (a maximum of 81 slots per hour)[17] and required airlines at those airports to use slots at least 80 percent of the time.[18] Since 2008, FAA has extended the duration of the orders imposing slot controls at JFK, LaGuardia, and Newark; they are now in effect until October 2013 or until DOT's Office of the Secretary and FAA issue a congestion management rule.[19] In April 2008, FAA proposed that the congestion management rule for LaGuardia include two different options for auctioning new or returned slots at LaGuardia whereby under one option, the agency would have kept the proceeds and under the second option, the proceeds would have gone to the incumbent carrier holding the slot.[20] In May 2008, FAA proposed applying such congestion management rules to JFK and Newark.[21] In October 2008, FAA published final congestion management rules for JFK, LaGuardia, and Newark assigning to existing operators the majority of slots at the airports and creating a market by annually auctioning off a limited number of slots in each of the first 5 years of the 10-year rule.[22] Before going into effect, on October 9, 2009, FAA rescinded[23] the final rules for the congestion management rules for JFK, LaGuardia, and Newark citing, among other things, that the rulemakings had been highly controversial, a court challenge, and a resulting December 2008 United States Court of Appeals for the District of Columbia Circuit ruling[24] that put on hold the implementation of the congestion management rules and their slot auction provisions.[25] In its rescission of the congestion management rules, FAA additionally cited fiscal year 2009 appropriations act legislation[26] providing, among other things, a statutory prohibition on using fiscal year 2009 funds to take any action regarding the auctioning of rights or permission to conduct airlines operations at U.S. commercial airports.[27] Subsequent to the rescission of the slot auction rules, FAA sought a dismissal of the case that was granted on October 14, 2009.[28]

In 2010, DOT's Office of the Secretary and FAA began drafting a "Slot Management and Transparency" rule for the New York City area airports.[29] According to DOT, this rulemaking would replace the current temporary orders limiting scheduled aircraft operations at JFK, LaGuardia, and Newark with a more permanent rule to address congestion and delay while also promoting fair access and competition. DOT's rulemaking is also aimed at ensuring that congestion and delay are minimized by limiting scheduled and unscheduled aircraft operations. Although the temporary orders prohibit the buying and selling of slots at the New York City area airports, according to DOT, the rulemaking would establish a secondary market for U.S. and foreign air carriers to buy, sell, trade, and lease slots at the three airports and "allow carriers serving or seeking to serve the New York area airports to exchange slots as their business models and strategic goals require." Under DOT's rulemaking schedule, the department was to provide the draft to the Office of Management and Budget for review by April 25, 2011, but as of July 2012, that had not yet occurred. At present, the High Density Rule applies only to Reagan National.

In 2009, Delta Air Lines and US Airways proposed trading slots that they held at LaGuardia and Reagan National, a trade that would allow Delta to establish a domestic hub at LaGuardia and US Airways to enhance its network at Reagan National.

The airlines sought FAA's permission because the transaction was considered a purchase of slots that, under the order limiting operations at LaGuardia, was not allowed. Under the proposal, Delta would transfer 42 slot pairs it held at Reagan National in exchange for 125 slot pairs at LaGuardia, among other provisions. DOT's Office of the Secretary and FAA granted the waiver request with conditions to counteract a substantial increase in market concentration by the two airlines that would result at those airports and to provide an opportunity for low cost airlines to compete, which required them to divest 14 pairs of slots at Reagan National and 20 pairs of slots at LaGuardia to new entrant and limited incumbent airlines (those holding less than 5 percent of slots at Reagan National and LaGuardia).[30] However, Delta and US Airways decided not to proceed with the transaction under these conditions.

In 2011, the two airlines reapplied for permission to exchange slots. Under the revised proposal, Delta would acquire 132 slot pairs (265 slots) at LaGuardia from US Airways and US Airways would acquire 42 slot pairs at LaGuardia from Delta, among other provisions. Delta would also pay US Airways $65 million. In their application, the two airlines said consumers would benefit from the transaction through, among other things, improved connectivity at LaGuardia and Reagan National and by using larger aircraft. DOT's Office of the Secretary and FAA approved the transaction and granted the waiver request from the temporary order's prohibition on purchasing slots, with conditions, citing expected consumer benefits and the increased presence of low cost airlines at LaGuardia and Reagan National since the previous application.[31]

The conditions required Delta and US Airways to divest to new entrants and limited incumbents fewer slots—8 slot pairs at Reagan National and 16 slot pairs at LaGuardia—than DOT's Office of the Secretary and FAA had required when they approved the first application. DOT's Office of the Secretary and FAA directed that the divested slots be sold through a bidding process, permitting Delta and US Airways to keep the proceeds. In 2011, Jet Blue purchased 8 slot pairs at LaGuardia for $32 million and 8 slot pairs at Reagan National for $40 million, and West Jet purchased 8 slot pairs at LaGuardia for $17.6 million.

Perimeter Rules Subject Airlines to Flight Distance Limitations to and from Reagan National and LaGuardia

Since the 1950s, the Port Authority of New York and New Jersey, which operates the New York City area airports, has had a rule limiting the distance of nonstop flights into and out of LaGuardia known as the perimeter rule. Until 1984, the perimeter rule was informal and prohibited nonstop flights into or out of LaGuardia to or from destinations more than 2,000 miles from the airport. In 1984, the Port Authority formally instituted a 1,500-mile perimeter rule but exempted service to Denver, which is more than 1,600 miles from LaGuardia, and flights on Saturdays.

In 1966, airlines at Reagan National voluntarily agreed to limit nonstop flights from the airport to destinations less than 650 miles away, with some exceptions. The Metropolitan Washington Airports Authority Act of 1986, enacted into law in October 1986, authorized the transfer of authority over Reagan National and Dulles from the federal government to the Metropolitan Washington Airports Authority, set Reagan National's perimeter rule at 1,250 miles, and prohibited the Airports Authority from increasing slot limits at Reagan National set in FAA's High Density Rule.[32] Two federal laws respectively enacted in 2000 and 2003 (the Wendell H. Ford Aviation Investment and Reform Act for the 21st Century[33] (AIR-21) and the Vision 100-Century of Aviation Reauthorization Act[34] (Vision 100)) enacted statutory modifications relating to the slot and perimeter rules at Reagan National. Among other things, AIR-21 required the Secretary of Transportation to grant 12 beyond perimeter and 12 within perimeter exemptions at Reagan National. Vision 100 amendments increased these numbers to 24 beyond perimeter exemptions and 20 within perimeter exemptions.[35] In effect, AIR-21 and Vision 100, combined, required the Secretary of Transportation to award 22 round trips, 12 with service to airports beyond the perimeter and 10 with service to airports within the perimeter.[36] In 2012, the FAA Modernization and Reform Act of 2012[37] was enacted into law, which reauthorized FAA, authorized 16 additional beyond perimeter exemptions at Reagan National comprised of eight within-perimeter flights to large hub airports to be converted to nonstop beyond-perimeter flights (four round-trips) and eight new additional nonstop beyond-perimeter flights (four round trips). With respect to the converted flights, under the 2012 act, each incumbent airline with 40 or more slots at Reagan National could convert one within-perimeter slot pair to one beyond-perimeter slot pair,[38] while the new beyond-perimeter slots were to be awarded to new entrants or airlines holding fewer than 40 slots. As the converted nonstop beyond-perimeter destinations, the incumbent airlines chose Los Angeles (American Airlines); Salt Lake City (Delta Air Lines); San Diego (US Airways); and San Francisco (United Airlines). Seven airlines applied for the four new beyond-perimeter slot pair exemptions, which, on May 14, 2012, DOT awarded to Alaska Airlines for Portland, Ore.; Jet Blue for San Juan, Puerto Rico; Southwest Airlines for Austin, Tex.; and Virgin America for San Francisco.

APPENDIX IV: TRENDS IN AVERAGE ANNUAL PASSENGER TRAFFIC AND AIRFARES AT SELECTED WASHINGTON, D.C., AREA AIRPORTS

Figures 8 through 31 below show the trends in average annual passenger traffic and airfares at Baltimore-Washington International Thurgood Marshall Airport (BWI) and Dulles International Airport (Dulles) for destinations granted beyond-perimeter slot exemptions at Reagan National Airport (Reagan National) under AIR-21 and Vision 100 between 2000 and 2004.

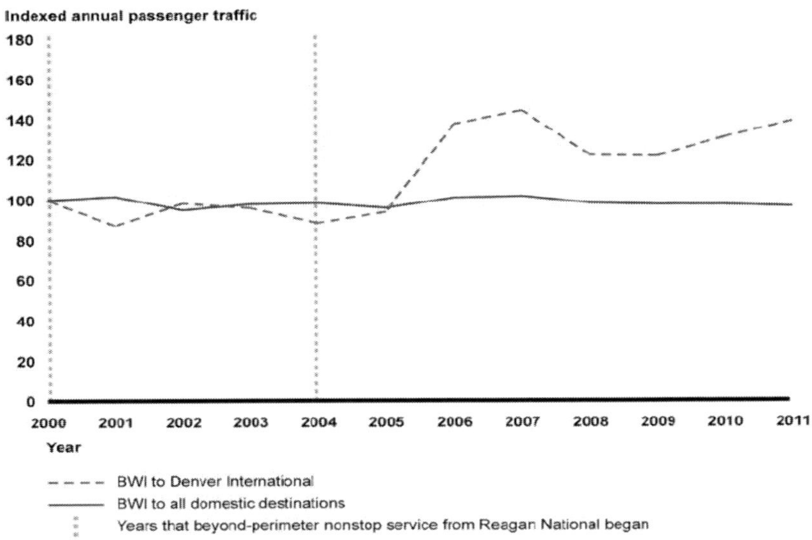

Source: GAO analysis of DOT data.

Figure 8. Indexed Average Passenger Traffic for All BWI Domestic Flights and Flights between BWI and Denver International Airport, 2000 to 2011.

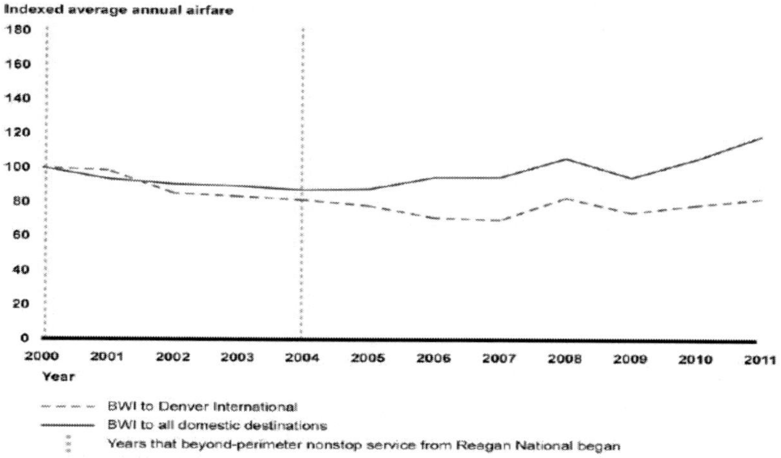

Source: GAO analysis of DOT data.

Figure 9. Indexed Average Annual Airfare for All BWI Domestic Flights and Flights between BWI and Denver International Airport, 2000 to 2011.

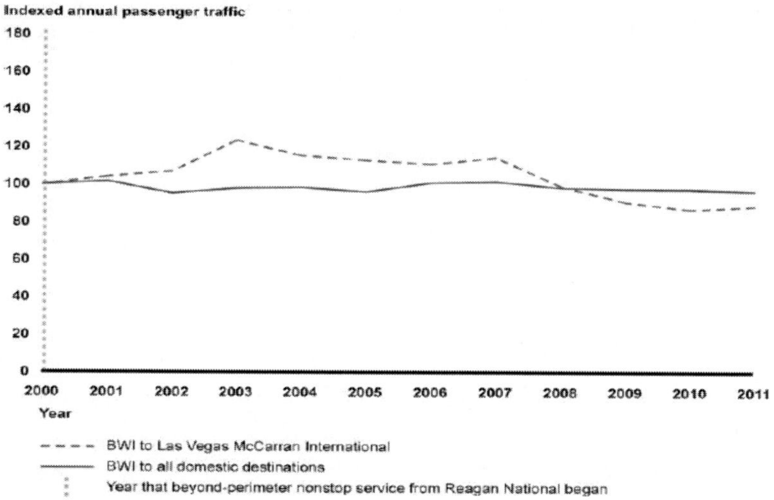

Source: GAO analysis of DOT data.

Figure 10. Indexed Average Annual Passenger Traffic for All BWI Domestic Flights and Flights between BWI and Las Vegas McCarran International Airport, 2000 to 2011.

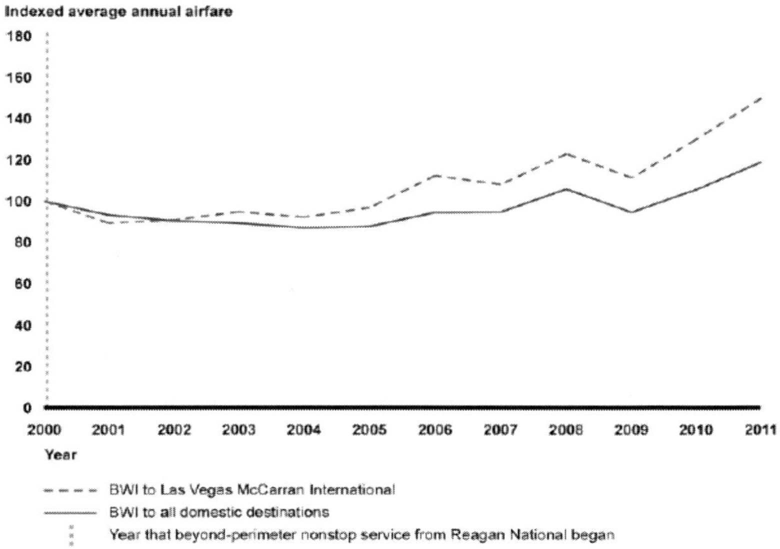

Source: GAO analysis of DOT data.

Figure 11. Indexed Average Annual Airfares for All BWI Domestic Flights and Flights between BWI and Las Vegas McCarran International Airport, 2000 to 2011.

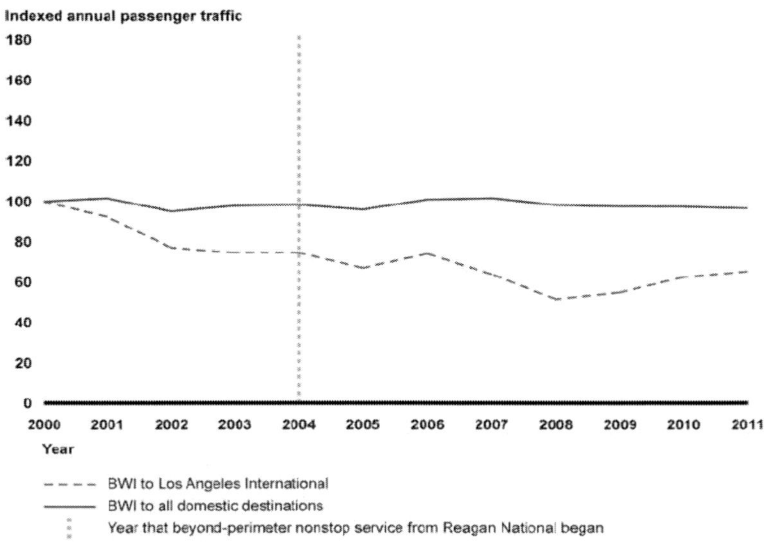

Source: GAO analysis of DOT data.

Figure 12. Indexed Average Passenger Traffic for All BWI Domestic Flights and Flights between BWI and Los Angeles International Airport, 2000 to 2011.

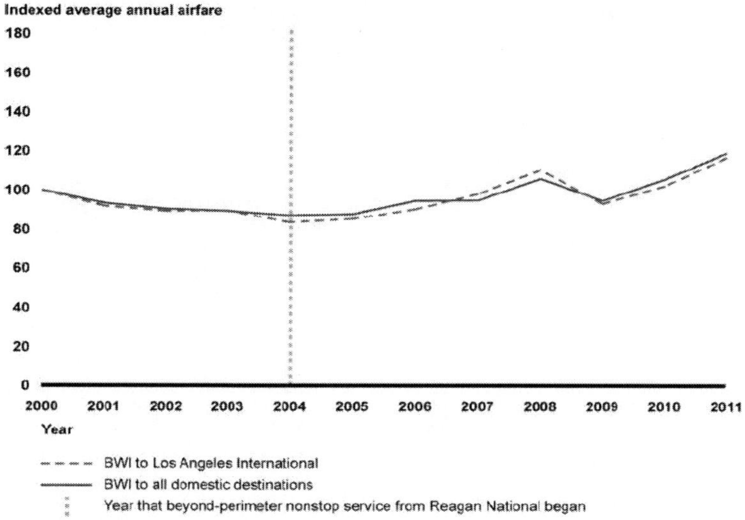

Source: GAO analysis of DOT data.

Figure 13. Indexed Average Annual Airfares for All BWI Domestic Flights and Flights between BWI and Los Angeles International Airport, 2000 to 2011.

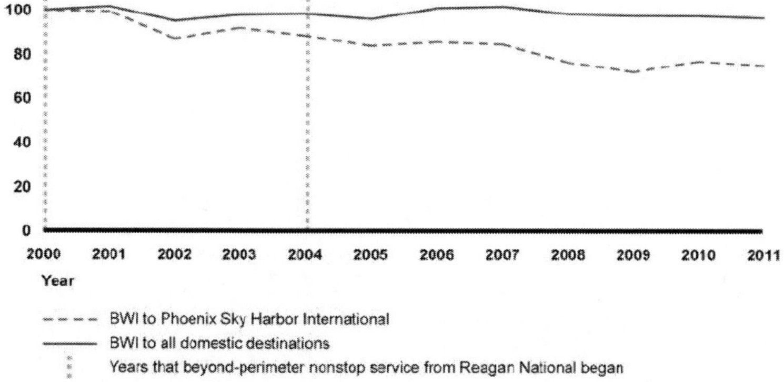

Source: GAO analysis of DOT data.

Figure 14. Indexed Average Passenger Traffic for All BWI Domestic Flights and Flights between BWI and Phoenix Sky Harbor International Airport, 2000 to 2011.

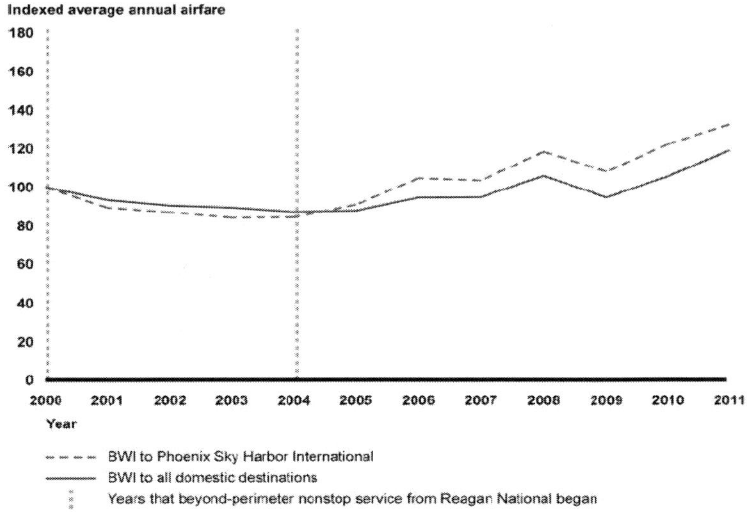

Source: GAO analysis of DOT data.

Figure 15. Indexed Average Airfares for All BWI Domestic Flights and Flights between BWI and Phoenix Sky Harbor International Airport, 2000 to 2011.

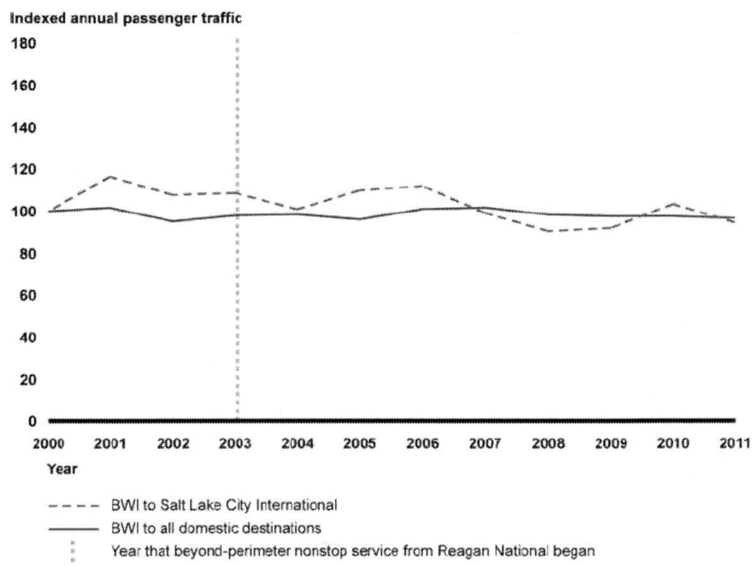

Source: GAO analysis of DOT data.

Figure 16. Indexed Average Passenger Traffic for All BWI Domestic Flights and Flights between BWI and Salt Lake City International Airport, 2000 to 2011.

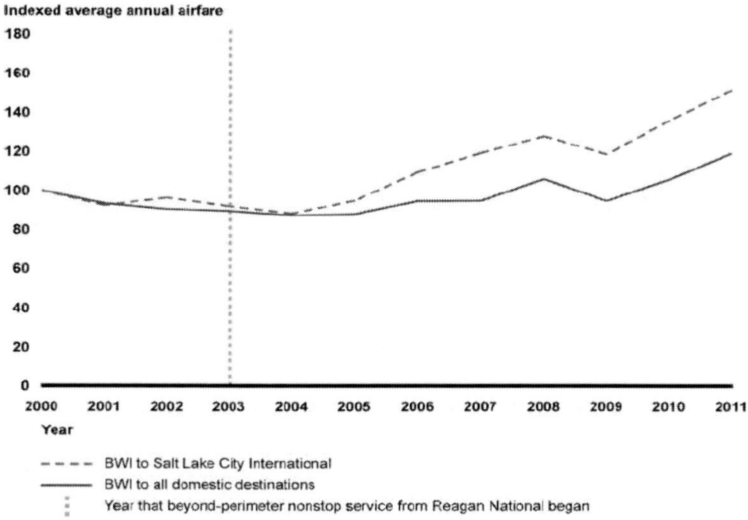

Source: GAO analysis of DOT data.

Figure 17. Indexed Average Airfares for All BWI Domestic Flights and Flights between BWI and Salt Lake City International Airport, 2000 to 2011.

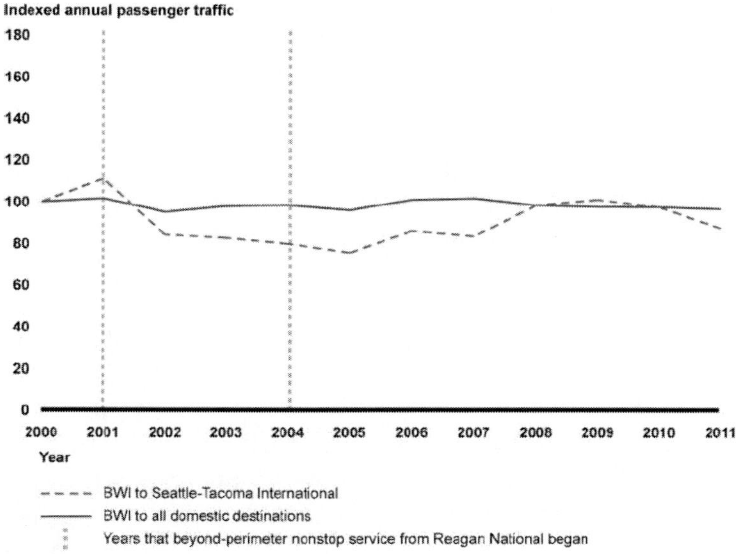

Source: GAO analysis of DOT data.

Figure 18. Indexed Average Passenger Traffic for All BWI Domestic Flights and Flights between BWI and Seattle-Tacoma International Airport, 2000 to 2011.

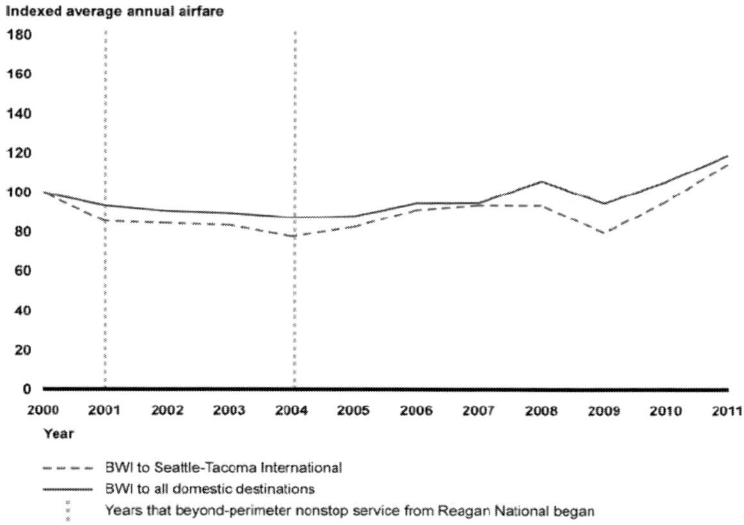

Source: GAO analysis of DOT data.

Figure 19. Indexed Average Airfares for All BWI Domestic Flights and Flights between BWI and Seattle-Tacoma International Airport, 2000 to 2011.

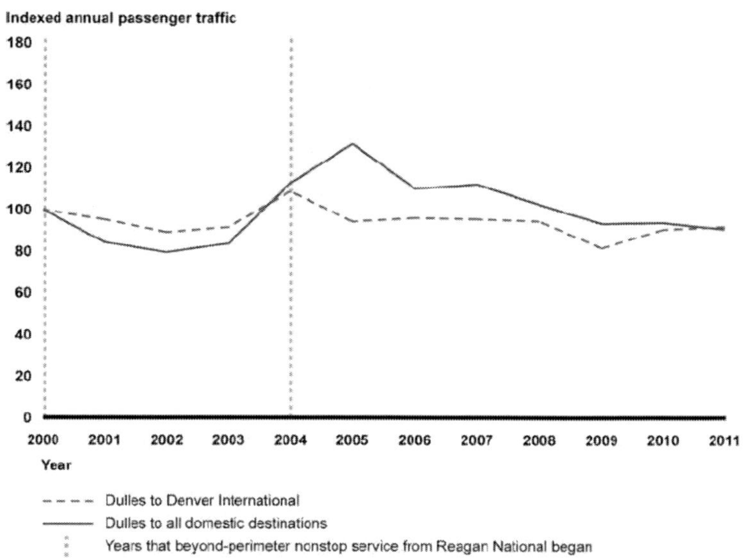

Source: GAO analysis of DOT data.

Figure 20. Indexed Average Passenger Traffic for All Dulles Domestic Flights and Flights between Dulles and Denver International Airport, 2000 to 2011.

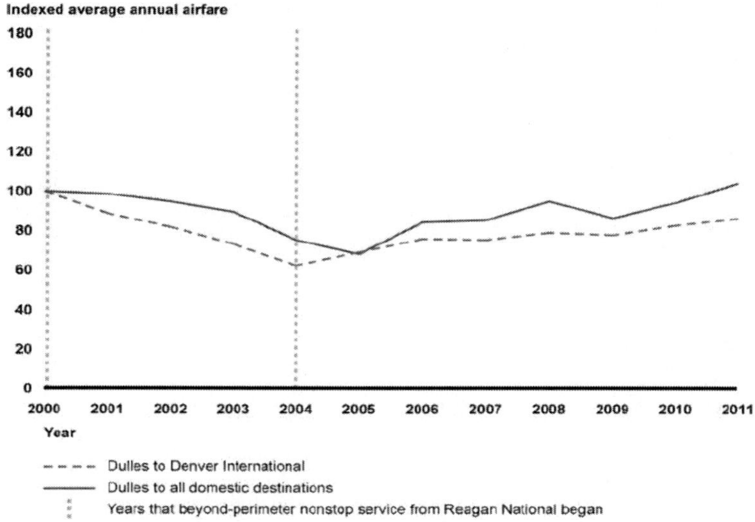

Source: GAO analysis of DOT data.

Figure 21. Indexed Average Airfares for All Dulles Domestic Flights and Flights between Dulles and Denver International Airport, 2000 to 2011.

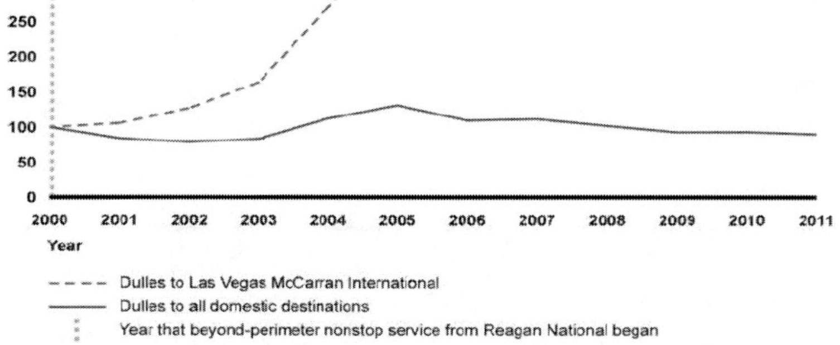

Source: GAO analysis of DOT data.

Figure 22. Indexed Average Annual Passenger Traffic for All Dulles Domestic Flights and Flights between Dulles and Las Vegas McCarran International Airport, 2000 to 2011.

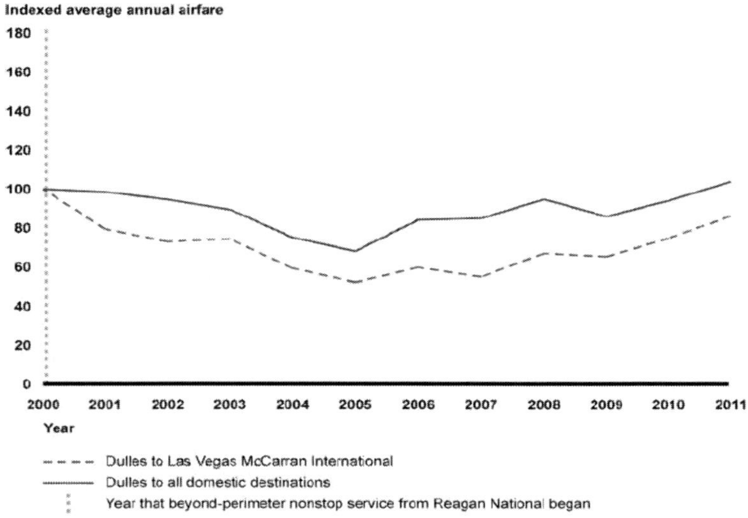

Source: GAO analysis of DOT data.

Figure 23. Indexed Average Annual Airfares for All Dulles Domestic Flights and Flights between Dulles and Las Vegas McCarran International Airport, 2000 to 2011.

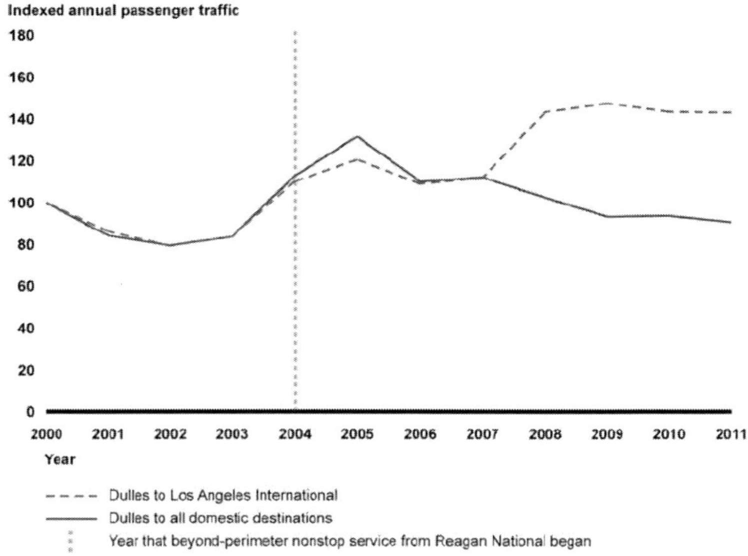

Source: GAO analysis of DOT data.

Figure 24. Indexed Average Annual Passenger Traffic for All Dulles Domestic Flights and Flights between Dulles and Los Angeles International Airport, 2000 to 2011.

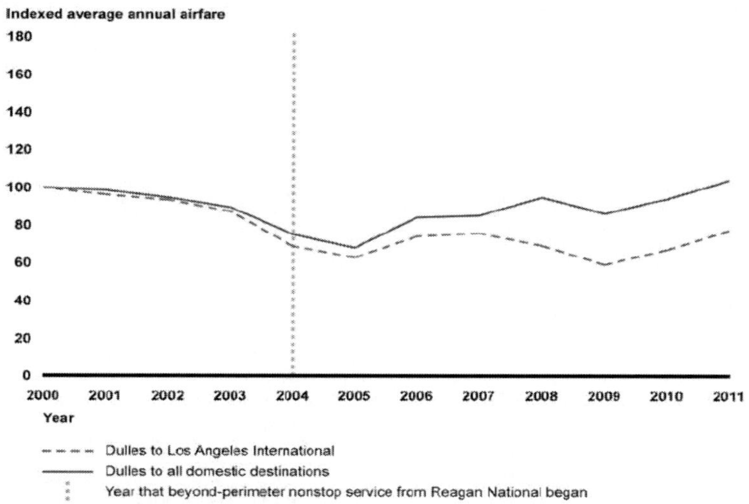

Source: GAO analysis of DOT data.

Figure 25. Indexed Average Annual Airfares for All Dulles Domestic Flights and Flights between Dulles and Los Angeles International Airport, 2000 to 2011.

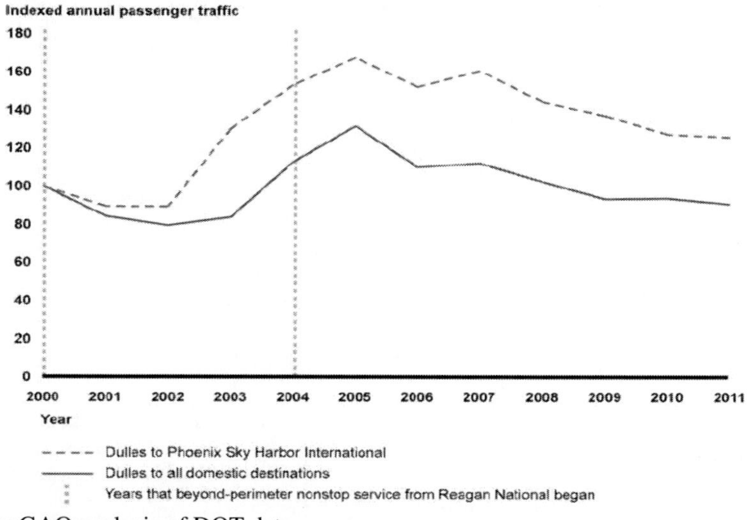

Source: GAO analysis of DOT data.

Figure 26. Indexed Average Annual Passenger Traffic for All Dulles Domestic Flights and Flights between Dulles and Phoenix Sky Harbor International Airport, 2000 to 2011.

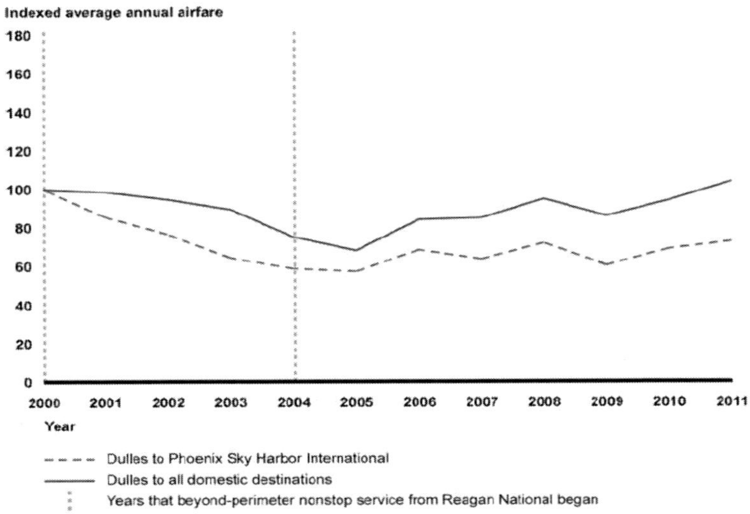

Source: GAO analysis of DOT data.

Figure 27. Indexed Average Annual Airfares for All Dulles Domestic Flights and Flights between Dulles and Phoenix Sky Harbor International Airport, 2000 to 2011.

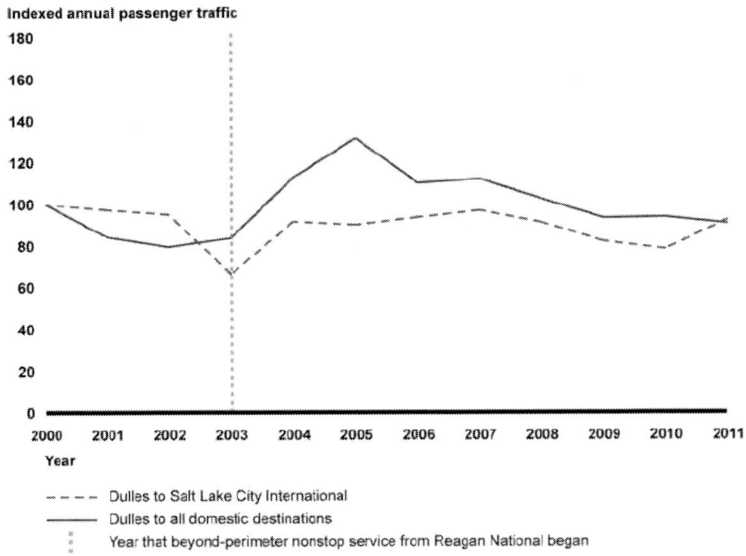

Source: GAO analysis of DOT data.

Figure 28. Indexed Average Annual Passenger Traffic for All Dulles Domestic Flights and Flights between Dulles and Salt Lake City International Airport, 2000 to 2011.

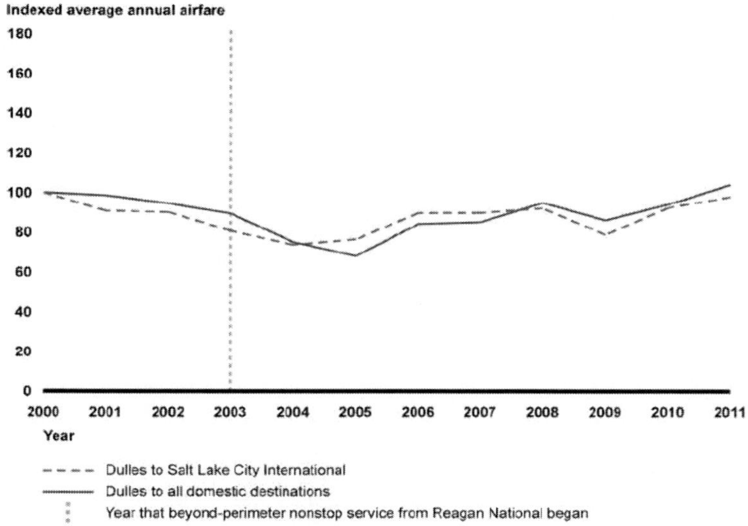

Source: GAO analysis of DOT data.

Figure 29. Indexed Average Airfares for All Dulles Domestic Flights and Flights between Dulles and Salt Lake City International Airport, 2000 to 2011.

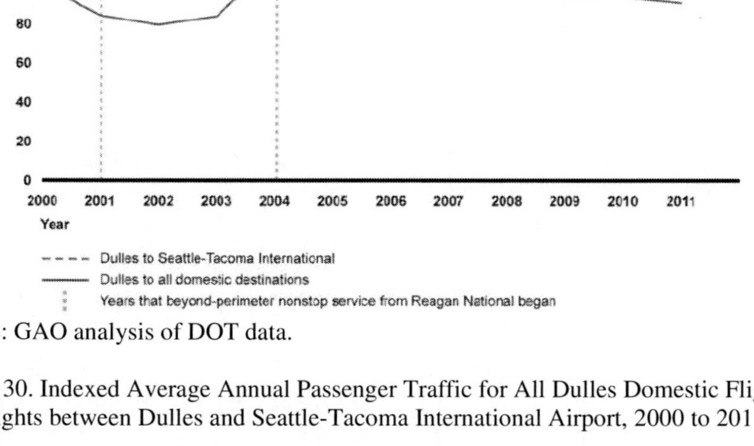

Source: GAO analysis of DOT data.

Figure 30. Indexed Average Annual Passenger Traffic for All Dulles Domestic Flights and Flights between Dulles and Seattle-Tacoma International Airport, 2000 to 2011.

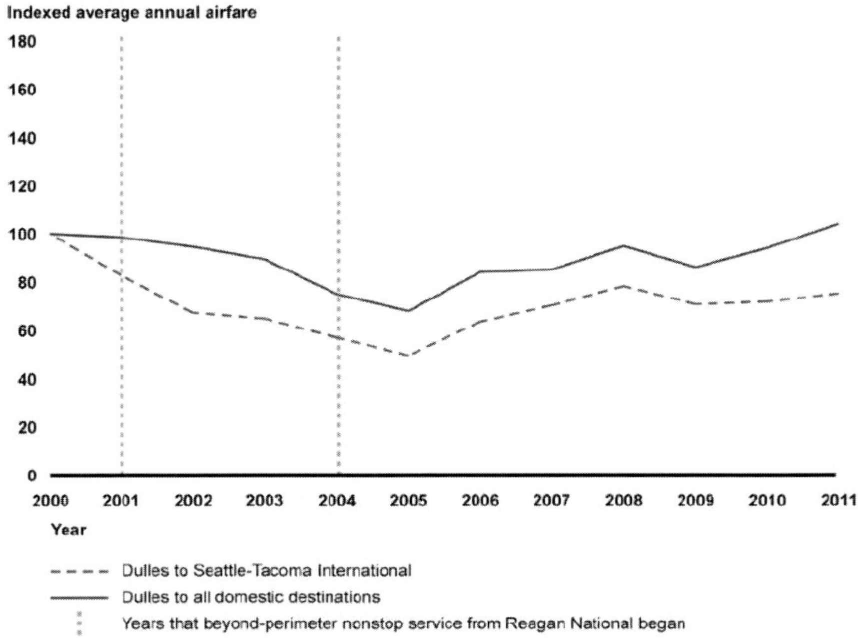

Source: GAO analysis of DOT data.

Figure 31. Indexed Average Annual Airfares for All Dulles Domestic Flights and Flights between Dulles and Seattle-Tacoma International Airport, 2000 to 2011.

APPENDIX V: LOGISTIC REGRESSION ANALYSIS OF SLOT-CONTROLLED AIRPORTS AND AIRCRAFT SIZE

The regression analysis explained in this appendix is designed to assess whether airlines tend to use smaller aircraft on flights to or from slot-controlled airports. The analysis is based on data for all scheduled passenger airline flights between large hub domestic airports for two different Thursdays (one in winter and one in summer) in 2011, and assesses whether and how several factors—including whether the flight is scheduled to arrive or depart a slot-controlled airport—are correlated with the use of smaller aircraft. For the base-case analysis we defined a smaller aircraft as ones with 100 seats or fewer. Specifically, this appendix discusses (1) the model hypothesis, (2) the conceptual framework of the model, (3) data source and variable definitions, and (4) base-case model results and sensitivity analyses.

Model Hypothesis

As discussed in the report, a variety of parties—airlines, the Port Authority of New York and New Jersey, and Department of Justice—assert that airlines currently operating out of slot-controlled airports use some of their slots in ways to keep out their competitors. One of these ways is using smaller aircraft, on average, at the four slot-controlled airports in an effort to meet the 80 percent usage rule.

Conceptual Framework of Model

As discussed in our report, we examined the number and proportion of scheduled passenger flights using smaller aircraft departing or arriving slot-controlled airports (which includes four airports) and the remaining 24 large hub airports.[1] In comparing flights arriving and departing the slot-controlled airports with other large hub airports that are not slot-controlled, we found that the four slot-controlled airports had a higher proportion of scheduled flights with smaller aircraft than flights to or from the remaining 24 large hub airports. We found that these differences are statistically significant.

Many factors may contribute to an airline's decision to use smaller aircraft, such as location and proximity to other major markets, restrictions on distance flown, the type of passengers being served, and the airline's route structure (e.g., a hub-and-spoke structure verses point-to-point). For example, all four of the slot-controlled airports are on the Eastern Seaboard of the United States with many destinations—large and small— within reasonably close proximity. Because shorter distance flights are generally served by smaller aircraft, flights to and from the slot-controlled airports may have a higher proportion of flights with small aircraft. Also, LaGuardia and Reagan National are subject to perimeter rules of 1,500 and 1,250 miles, respectively, that limits the distance of flights from these airports. A restriction on flight distance such as this would likely skew aircraft use toward smaller sized craft. Whether an airport being served is a business versus leisure (tourist) market may also affect the size of aircraft—for example, flights serving leisure markets may tend to use larger aircraft less frequently than a business market. And finally, an airline's route structure could influence the distance of flights or aircraft size—for example, an airport that serves as a hub for an airline will require more short distance flights than a point-to-point business model.

Since a variety of factors in addition to slot controls may be correlated with the use of a small aircraft, we developed a logistic regression model that controls for other factors that may be correlated with aircraft size. To isolate the correlation between flights arriving or departing slot-controlled airports and aircraft size, we defined aircraft as small if its capacity was 100 seats or fewer.[2] We applied a logistic regression technique (or logit model) in which the scheduled flights are defined as using small aircraft (100 seats or fewer) or large (more than 100 seats), and assessed how each of a set of independent factors (including whether the flights arrives or departs a slot-controlled airport) correlates with the odds of a small aircraft used on that flight. All factors related to aircraft size may not be fully controlled for by this model. Also, as with any regression model, this analysis does not prove a causal relationship between aircraft size and slot-controlled airport, only the correlation between the two.

Data Source and Variables

The primary data source for the model is airlines' schedule data from Innovata, which provides information on all airlines scheduled flights. The level of observation for this analysis is each individually scheduled passenger flight. We used all flights between the 28 large hub airports[3] on two Thursdays in 2011—February 10, 2011, and August 11, 2011—for a total of 13,901 flights. Thursdays are generally considered to be a high-demand day, and February and August are representative months for the winter and summer seasons, respectively. The schedule data provide relevant information for each flight, including the size of aircraft, the date and time of the scheduled flight, the origin and destination airport, and the marketing and operating airline.

Dependent Variable

The dependent variable for the analysis is a dummy (or indicator) variable—that is, a variable that takes a value of one or zero depending on the presence or absence of some characteristic. In this case, the dependent variable takes the value of one if the scheduled flight uses a small aircraft size (100 or fewer seats) and the value of zero if the flight uses a large aircraft (greater than 100 seats).

Independent Variables[4]

Slot-controlled airport (variable of interest): A dummy variable that takes the value of one if either the origin or destination of the flight is a slot-controlled airport. We used several different slot-controlled airport dummy variables, including one for all four slot-controlled airports as a group (slot4), one for only the three New York City area slot-controlled airports (slot3) and one for each individual slot-controlled airport alone.

Legacy airline: A dummy variable that takes the value of one if the flight is marketed by one of the legacy airlines we defined (Delta Air Lines, United Airlines, American Airlines, US Airways, and Continental Airlines) and takes the value of zero for all other marketing airlines. Airlines vary in their fleet mix. Some airlines—either on their own or through partnerships with other airlines—operate a varied fleet mix with both large and small aircraft, while other airlines tend to fly only a few aircraft types that may have little variation in the size of aircraft. We expect that when the marketing airline is a legacy airline, all else equal, there is a greater propensity to use smaller aircraft because these airlines and their partners tend to deploy a wide range of aircraft size, including many commuter-sized aircraft, across a broad range of types of routes.

Flight distance: A categorical variable that is derived from distance quartiles of the flights analyzed. The four distance categories are less than 325 miles, 325 to 602 miles, 603 to 998 miles, and greater than 998 miles. Flight distance is a key factor in the decision underlying the assignment of aircraft to flights. We used the flights that fell into the second quartile (325 miles to 602 miles in distance) as the reference category that the other flight distance dummy variables are compared to. We expect that shorter flights would tend to use smaller aircraft.

Flight frequency for an airline route: A categorical variable indicating the importance of a particular route to an airline's operations. We define flight frequency on an airline's route as the total number of flights operated by the same airline on a given day from the same origin to the same destination. Few frequencies on an airline's route indicate that the route may not be highly connected to the airline's network, while numerous frequencies indicate a greater degree of connection, possibly involving one of the airline's hub airports.[5] We divided the number of flights on an airline's route into quartiles and used the two lower quartiles (which together included all airlines' routes with fewer than 6 flights per day) as reference categories that the remaining two quartiles are compared to. The third quartile includes airlines' routes with 6 to 8 flights and day and the fourth quartile includes routes with 9 or more flights per day. We expect that greater dedication to serving a route (higher flight frequency) will be correlated with reduced odds of using a small aircraft.

Tourism: A dummy variable that takes the value of one if either the origin or destination of a flight is one of three cities that have substantial tourist travel (Las Vegas, Nevada; Orlando, Florida; and Fort Lauderdale, Florida) based on hotel revenues relative to population and our judgment about which cities have substantial tourist travel. We defined Las Vegas McCarran International, Orlando International, and Fort Lauderdale-Hollywood International airports as the three tourism-oriented airports in the analysis. We expect that smaller aircraft will be less likely to be used on flights to and from these airports.

Base-Case Model Results and Sensitivity Analysis

Table 7 provides results of our base-case model that defines a small aircraft as one with 100 seats or fewer. The results are expressed as odds ratios, which represents the odds that a flight uses a small aircraft (100 seats or fewer) divided by the odds that a flight uses a large aircraft (more than 100 seats).

Table 7. Logistic Regression Results for Slot-Controlled-Airport and Aircraft-Size Model, Small Aircraft with 100 Seats or Fewer

Variable	Odds ratio[a]
To or from any of the four slot-controlled airports	1.75
To or from tourism airport	0.16
Marketed by a legacy airline	8.71
6 to 8 flights per day by same airline from same origin to same destination	0.32
9 or more flights per day by same airline from same origin to same destination	0.11
Flight distance less than 325 miles	3.99
Flight distance between 603 and 998 miles	0.40
Flight distance more than 998 miles	0.06

Source: GAO analysis of airline schedule data

[a]All odds ratios are significant at the p-value <0.01 (1 percent level). The significance of the coefficients in the models was evaluated using a simple Wald test statistic, which is asymptotically equivalent to the likelihood-ratio chi-square statistic. The percentage of flights correctly predicted by the model to be on small versus larger aircraft was 85-percent. The measure is known as the concordance rate.

The odds ratio for the variable of interest (slot4) is greater than 1, indicating that a flight to or from any of the four slot-controlled airports is more likely to use a small aircraft than a flight to or from the other 24 large hub airports that are not slot-controlled.[6] Specifically, the odds that a flight to or from a slot-controlled airport uses a smaller aircraft is 75 percent higher than the odds for a flight to and from the other 24 large hub airports that are not slot-controlled. This result and the odds ratios for all other variable in the base-case scenario are statistically significant.

In addition to the model discussed above, we also ran with the model with alternative definitions of the slot-controlled-airport dummy variable. Table 8 shows the odds ratios from these 5 addition model runs for the variously defined slot-controlled-airport variable. The results for the independent variables in these model runs were reasonably stable both in the direction and magnitude of the odds ratios.

Table 8. Logistic Regression Results for Alternative Slot-Controlled-Airport Variable Definitions, Small Aircraft with 100 Seats or Fewer

Slot-controlled-airport variable	Odds Ratio
To or from any of the three New York City area slot-controlled airports	1.68[a]
To or from LaGuardia	2.08[a]
To or from JFK	1.63[a]
To or from Newark	1.22[b]
To or from Reagan National	1.72[a]

[a]Indicates odds ratio is significant at a p-value > 0.01.
[b]Indicates odds ratio is significant at a p-value < 0.1.

We also conducted sensitivity analyses by testing two alternative definitions for small aircraft. We ran the same models described above, but defined a small aircraft as (1) aircraft with 124 seats or fewer (which is the median aircraft size for this data set) and (2) aircraft with 80 seats or fewer (which excludes the largest regional jets). Tables 9 and 10 show the results of these model runs, including the results for each of the six different slot-controlled airport dummy variable definitions. All other independent variables included in the models were robust—both in terms of the direction, magnitude, and statistical significance of odds ratios— across the three definitions for small aircraft.

In addition, the odds ratios for all definitions of the slot-controlled-airport dummy variable are greater than 1—indicating a greater odds of a flight using a small aircraft to or from the slot-controlled airport, however the slot variable was defined. The magnitude of the odds ratio, however, varies based on the definition of a small aircraft (that is, a cutoff of 80, 100, or 124 seats). Also, the degree of the statistical significance of the odds ratios for Newark and JFK vary. The odds ratio for Newark becomes more significant under the alternative aircraft definitions (i.e., a cutoff of 80 or 124 seats). And, while odds ratio for the JFK dummy variable was significant in both the base case (100-seat cutoff) and the 124-seat cutoff, the odds ratio for JFK is not statistically significant in the 80 seat cutoff.

Table 9. Logistic Regression Results for Alternative Slot-Controlled-Airport Variable Definitions, Small Aircraft with 124 Seats or Fewer

Slot-controlled airport variable	Odds Ratio
To or from any of the four slot-controlled airports	2.49[a]
To or from any of the three New York City area slot-controlled airports	2.18[a]
To or from LaGuardia	3.68[a]
To or from JFK	1.53[a]
To or from Newark	1.48[a]
To or from Reagan National	4.29[a]

Source: GAO analysis of airline schedule data

[a]Indicates odds ratio is significant at p-value < 0.01.

Table 10. Logistic Regression Results for Alternative Slot-Controlled-Airport Variable Definitions, Small Aircraft with 80 Seats or Fewer

Slot-controlled airport variable	Odds Ratio
To or from any of the four slot-controlled airports	1.55[a]
To or from any of the three New York City area slot-controlled airports	1.61[a]
To or from LaGuardia	2.17[a]
To or from JFK	1.22
To or from Newark	1.26[b]
To or from Reagan National	1.41[a]

Source: GAO analysis of airline schedule data

[a]Indicates odds ratio is significant at p-value < 0.01. [b]Indicates odds ratio is significant at p-value < 0.05.

End Notes

[1] FAA regulations at 14 C.F.R. Part 93, subparts K and S applicable to Reagan National Airport use the term "slots," whereas FAA orders applicable to JFK, LaGuardia, and Newark use the term "operating authorization." For the purposes of this report we refer to both as slots.

[2] FAA Modernization and Reform Act of 2012, Pub. L. No. 112-95, § 414, 126 Stat. 11 (2012).

[3] GAO, *Reagan National Airport: Capacity to Handle Additional Flights and Impact on Other Airports,* GAO/RCED-99-234 (Washington, D.C.: Sept. 17, 1999) and *Reagan National Airport: Update on Capacity to Handle Flights and Impact on Other Airports*, GAO-07-352 (Washington, D.C.: Feb. 28, 2007).

[4] 74 Fed. Reg. 52132 (Oct. 9, 2009); 74 Fed. Reg. 52134 (Oct. 9, 2009). The federal court ruling was an order by the United States Court of Appeals for the District of Columbia Circuit. *Port Authority of New York and New Jersey v. Federal Aviation Administration*, Court of Appeals for the District of Columbia, Order No. 08-1329 (Dec. 8, 2008).

[5] Federal law defines large hub airports as those commercial service airports that have at least 1 percent of the passenger boardings. 49 U.S.C. § 40102(29).

[6] BTS defines these airports as those within the continental United States that enplaned 1 percent or more of the domestic scheduled-service passengers as of June 2010. Federal law defines large hub airports as those commercial service airports that have at least 1 percent of the passenger boardings. 49 U.S.C. § 40102(29).

[7] The data indicated that the cancellation rate at LaGuardia was generally twice the system-wide average during this period. See also GAO, *National Airspace System: DOT and FAA Actions Will Likely Have a Limited Effect on Reducing Delays during Summer 2008 Travel Season,* GAO-08-934T (Washington, D.C.: July 15, 2008).

[8] In 1998, Washington National Airport was renamed Ronald Reagan Washington National Airport.

[9] In 2009, FAA reduced the operating limits at LaGuardia to 71 scheduled operations per hour to improve operational efficiency. The current slot allocations were kept, but any slots returned to FAA, withdrawn for non-use, or unallocated during each affected hour would be retired until the number of slots in that hour reaches 71.

[10] Slots are subject to FAA withdrawal, for example, if a slot is not used at least 80 percent of the time over the applicable time period. In addition, slots are subject to FAA withdrawal at any time to meet operational needs such as reduced airport capacity.

[11] Although airlines consider slots to be valuable assets, FAA slot regulations at 14 C.F.R. § 93.223(a), for example, provide that slots do not represent a property right but represent an operating privilege subject to absolute FAA control. The FAA slot regulations applicable to Reagan National also provide, in general, that slots may be bought, sold, leased, or traded for slots at other slot controlled airports. 14 C.F.R. § 93.221(a).

[12] Under FAA's temporary order applicable to LaGuardia, slots are not allocated on Saturdays.

[13] The summer season runs from the fourth Sunday in March to the fourth Saturday in October. The winter season runs from the fourth Sunday in October to the fourth Saturday in March.

[14] See, e.g., 73 Fed. Reg. 3510, 3513-14 (Jan. 18, 2008). In comparison to the temporary FAA orders in place at the New York City area airports, the FAA High Density Rule regulations applicable to slots at Reagan National provide, in part, that except as otherwise provided, slots may be bought, sold, or leased. 14 C.F.R. § 93.221. The major exception to this regulation at Reagan National is that slot exemptions may not be bought, sold, leased, or otherwise transferred, except through an air carrier merger or acquisition. 49 U.S.C. 41714(j).

[15] Pub. L. No. 111-8, Division I, Title I, §115, 123 Stat. 524, 921 (2009). The Omnibus Appropriations Act, 2009 contained a provision prohibiting the Secretary of Transportation from using such fiscal year 2009 appropriations to promulgate regulations or take any action regarding the scheduling of airline operations at any commercial airport in the U.S. if such regulation or action involved, among other things, auctioning or rights or permission to conduct airline operations, the implementation of peak-period pricing or other forms of congestion pricing, withdrawing a right or permission to conduct operations at such an airport, or requiring a carrier to transfer involuntarily any such right or permission to another.

[16] From 1986 to 2006, when FAA managed congestion at JFK and LaGuardia under the High Density Rule, airlines were allowed to buy and sell slots at these airports. However, in comments to FAA on a proposed congestion management rule for LaGuardia, some airlines indicated that a secondary market did not develop because the Wendell H. Ford Aviation Investment and Reform Act for the 21st Century (AIR-21) granted exemptions from the High Density Rule's flight restrictions to some airlines for free.

[17] The perimeter rule for LaGuardia provides an exception for nonstop flights to and from Denver because there was existing service to Denver when the rule went into effect.

[18] Pub. L. No. 99-500, 100 Stat. 1783, 1783-375 (1986); Pub. L. No. 99-591, 100 Stat. 3341, 3341-376 (1986).

[19] Pub. L. No. 106-181, 114 Stat. 61 (2000).

[20] Pub. L. No. 108-176, 117 Stat. 2490 (2003).

[21] The statutes also authorized 20 additional slot exemptions within the 1,250-mile perimeter.

[22] Pub. L. No. 112-95, 126 Stat. 11 (2012).

[23] MITRE, an FAA contractor, conducted this analysis in August 2011. For information about how MITRE analyzes airport capacity, see Appendix V of GAO, *National Airspace System: Setting On-Time Performance Targets at Congested Airports Could Help Focus FAA's Actions,* GAO-10-542 (Washington, D.C.: May 26, 2010).

[24] Based on an FAA analysis of unscheduled operations from May through August 2011 indicating that there was an average of 17.3 daily general aviation operations weekdays from 6:00 a.m. to 10:59 p.m. We reported in 2007 that there were about 200 general aviation and unscheduled flights at Reagan National in 2006, or an average of one-half of a flight operation per day. The number of general aviation and unscheduled flights has increased at Reagan National since 2006 in part because TSA updated security procedures that made more general aviation flights possible, for example, by expanding the number of airports from which flights can emanate.

[25] From 4 p.m. to 4:59 p.m., the number of slot allocations will increase from 52 to 54, and from 5 p.m. to 5:59 p.m. and from 6 p.m. to 6:59 p.m., the number of slot allocations will increase from 51 to 53.

[26] Based on an FAA analysis of general aviation and unscheduled weekday operations from May through August 2011.

[27] Three slots each were available at 6:00 a.m. and 10:00 p.m. and 40 were available at 11:00 p.m. These numbers exclude other slots that are allocated on an ad hoc day-of basis following a request from the operator and one commuter slot that is available at 9:00 p.m. and another at 10:00 p.m. that are allocated on a temporary basis and subject to recall by FAA.

[28] The official said that although these airlines need the same type of space to function, e.g., ticket counters, gates, and baggage systems, each airline needs a different amount of space, so economies of scale cannot always be maximized.

[29] Transportation Research Board of the National Academies, *Reference Guide on Understanding Common Use at Airports,* (Washington, D.C.: 2010).

[30] We asked TSA to assess the impact of the new beyond-perimeter flights on wait times using its security screening throughput model. As inputs to the model, we provided TSA with the flight times for the new beyond-perimeter flights, data on the maximum number of passengers on those flights, and the screening checkpoints that the passengers would use. Although the results from this model suggested that any increase in wait times at Reagan National would be minimal, we are not reporting the precise estimates of wait time changes because they would imply a greater level of precision than the model could reasonably provide.

[31] National Capital Region Transportation Planning Board and Metropolitan Washington Council of Governments, Draft *2011 Washington-Baltimore Regional Air Passenger Survey*, (Washington, D.C.: May 2011).

[32] In calculating the maximum number of enplanements, we included the eight new daily beyond-perimeter departures and assumed that each daily flight used the aircraft specified in the airline's application for the slot exemption and that those aircraft were 100 percent full. We did not include the passenger impact of the within-perimeter flights that were converted to beyond-perimeter slot exemptions because there were too many unknown factors, such as whether the passengers on those flights were connecting or originating at Reagan National or the load factors on them.

[33] In 1981, FAA adopted rules to implement FAA's Metropolitan Washington Airports' policy (45 Fed. Reg. 62398 (Sept. 18, 1980)) to guide the future operations and development of Reagan National and Dulles. This implementing Metropolitan Washington Airport rule provided, among other things, that the perimeter rule would maintain the long-haul nonstop service at Dulles and be consistent with the roles proposed for Reagan National as a short/medium-haul facility and for Dulles as an unrestricted facility available for all types of operations. 48 Fed. Reg. 58036 (Nov. 27, 1981). In 1986, the federal law creating MWAA provided that the regulations of MWAA's predecessor agency shall become the regulations of MWAA. Pub. L. No. 99-500, 100 Stat. 1783, 1783-375 (1986); Pub. L. No. 99-591, 100 Stat. 3341, 3341-376 (1986).

[34] The 2005 example involved Frontier Airlines and the 2012 example involved Delta Air Lines.

[35] Cost per enplaned passenger is defined as all landing fees, airside usage charges, fuel flowage fees, terminal rents, and other terminal payments to an airport, divided by the number of enplaned passengers. We did not assess the possible impact of the new beyond-perimeter flights on the cost per enplaned passenger at BWI because of differences in how airport authorities calculate those numbers. Airlines use cost per enplaned passenger as a standardized measure of relative unit costs to compare costs among airports.

[36] For comparison purposes, MWAA provided data showing that the costs per enplaned passenger was substantially higher at Dulles than at most other large hub airports. However, these data were not directly comparable because airports vary in terms of what airlines and airports pay for, which affects the costs per enplanement.

[37] Federal Aviation Administration, *Terminal Area Forecast Summary, Fiscal Years 2011- 2040.*

[38] According to Moody's Investors Service, Inc., MWAA is among five U.S. airport authorities with the most debt. In 2011, MWAA incurred $222 million in interest expense.

[39] The automated passenger train system at Dulles, called Aerotrain, is separate from the project to extend Metrorail to Dulles. MWAA aviation funds are responsible for 4.1 percent of the total cost of the Metrorail extension to Dulles. However, according to MWAA, all bonds for

the corridor project are backed by a separate MWAA toll road credit that is firewalled from the MWAA's aviation credit.

[40] According to an MWAA official, debt is not issued on an airport-by-airport basis; but rather as airport-system revenue-bond debt for both airports. However, MWAA tracks where the debt proceeds are applied by airport.

[41] MWAA receives revenues from landing fees, which are based on aircraft weight; airport leases with airlines; and concessions. Although non-aeronautical revenues, such as concessions, are not maintained separately by airport, MWAA officials said revenues are not sufficient to cover much debt.

[42] Pub. L. No. 112-95, 126 Stat. 11, 92 (2012).

[43] FAA supports airports' efforts to mitigate aviation noise mainly through its voluntary noise compatibility program, known as the Part 150 Noise Compatibility Program, which provides guidance to airports on how to develop noise compatibility plans to mitigate noise on and around airports. MWAA last conducted a noise compatibility study on Reagan National in 2004. See also the forthcoming GAO report, *Airport Noise Grants: FAA Needs to Better Ensure Project Eligibility and Improve Strategic Goal and Performance Measures*, GAO-12-890.

[44] Slot controls are one type of demand management measure used to help manage congestion. Other demand management measures include congestion pricing and slot auctions.

[45] Wendell H. Ford Aviation Investment and Reform Act for the 21st Century (AIR-21), Pub. L. No. 106-181 (2000). AIR-21 mandated that the High Density Rule slot controls would no longer apply to JFK and LaGuardia after January 2007. The exemptions for new entrant airlines and for service to small communities using regional jets at JFK and LaGuardia were interim measures until the AIR-21 slot related phase-out became effective.

[46] In announcing its intent to limit the number of slot exemptions allowed to operate at LaGuardia, FAA noted language in section 231 of AIR-21 providing, in general, that AIR-21's slot phase out provisions shall not be construed to affect FAA's authority for safety and the movement of air traffic. 65 Fed. Reg. 69126 (Nov. 15, 2000). FAA explained that under its authority for safety and the movement of air traffic, and pending the development of a longer term solution, it sought to temporarily cap AIR-21 slot exemptions at LaGuardia. This limit, according to FAA, still allowed a significant increase in operations at the airport above the regulatory limits, thus serving congressional objectives while stretching capacity to its practical limits. 71 Fed. Reg. 51360 (Aug. 29, 2006).

[47] FAA and its federally funded research and development center, the MITRE Corporation's Center for Advanced Aviation System Development, used a model that estimated the level of delay associated with various levels of operations at both JFK and Newark airports.

[48] Because our analysis did not assess the behavior of individual airlines, we could not determine the prevalence of this practice among airlines. See appendix V for a detailed discussion of our analysis and the results.

[49] FAA officials told us that some additional operations have been added in less desirable hours.

[50] According to DOT and enforcement case precedent, airlines may not routinely cancel flights for economic reasons. This practice, according to DOT, would constitute an unfair method of competition to engage in "unrealistic scheduling of flights" identified in 14 C.F.R. § 399.81 as an unfair or deceptive practice. See, DOT Order 97-1-6, Bellair Incorporated (Jan. 13, 1997).

[51] Under specified circumstances, FAA may waive the 80 percent usage requirement. For example, with respect to JFK, LaGuardia, and Newark, FAA may waive the usage requirement "in the event of a highly unusual and unpredictable condition which is beyond

the control of the carrier and which affects carrier operations for a period of five consecutive days or more." Waiver provisions applicable to Reagan National require such a condition to exist for a period of 9 or more days. 76 Fed. Reg. 18616 (Apr. 4, 2011); 76 Fed. Reg. 18618 (Apr. 4, 2011); 76 Fed. Reg. 18620 (Apr. 4, 2011); 14 C.F.R. § 93.227.

[52] Although airlines might consider slots to be valuable assets, FAA slot regulations at 14 C.F.R. § 93.223(a), for example, provide that slots do not represent a property right but represent an operating privilege subject to absolute FAA control.

[53] To conduct this analysis, we compared the total number of scheduled flights for each of 7 days in February 2011 and each of 7 days in August 2011 with daily slot allocation numbers provided by FAA for each slot-controlled airport.

[54] Specifically, we found that one or more airlines at Newark scheduled less than 80 percent of their allocated slots for selected Saturdays in the 2011 summer season. We calculated schedule data for the third Saturday of each month of the summer season (April, May, June, July, August, September, and October), which represented 7 of the 30 Saturdays during the 2011 summer season. FAA officials said that the third week of each month is most representative of the rest of the month. Of the 7 Saturdays that we examined, schedule rates were between 66 percent and 77 percent. Given average cancellation rates for Newark and the typical scheduling rates observed for the days that we examined, it is practically impossible (though theoretically possible) for all airlines to have met the 80 percent usage requirement for all slots on Saturdays in the 2011 summer season at Newark.

[55] This practice is also common at slot-controlled outside the United States and required under the Worldwide Slot Guidelines. The returned slots do not count against the airline's usage rate, so long as they are returned before the handback deadline, which is about 10 weeks before the start of the season.

[56] See, DOJ, *Comments of the United States Department of Justice on Notice of Petition for Waiver of the Terms of the Order Limiting Scheduled Operations at LaGuardia Airport and Solicitation of Comments on Grant of Petition with Conditions,* (Washington, D.C.: Mar. 24, 2010).

[57] At the New York City area airports, FAA may waive the 80 percent requirement in the event of a highly unusual and unpredictable condition which is beyond the control of the carrier and which affects carrier operations for a period of 5 consecutive days or more. The provision applicable to Reagan National provides that such period must be for 9 or more days. This provision further provides examples of conditions which could justify waiver – weather conditions which result in the restricted operation of an airport for an extended period of time or the grounding of an aircraft type.

[58] In April 2008, FAA published a supplemental congestion-management rule proposal for LaGuardia without the minimum aircraft size requirement. 75 Fed. Reg. 20846 (Apr. 17, 2008). The final rule for the Congestion Management Rule for LaGuardia, based on the supplemental proposal, was issued in October 2008 and rescinded in 2009.

[59] See, Department of Justice, *Comments of the United States Department of Justice on Notice of Petition for Waiver of the Terms of the Order Limiting Scheduled Operations at LaGuardia Airport and Solicitation of Comments on Grant of Petition with Conditions,* (Washington, D.C.: Mar. 24, 2010). In an analysis of aircraft size, DOJ controlled for the fact that commuter slots at Reagan National come with a restriction as to the size of the aircraft that can be flown.

[60] For the purpose of this report, we defined "small" aircraft as one that contains 100 seats or fewer. We also examined flights for which a "small" aircraft was smaller than or equal in

size to the median-sized aircraft (124 seats) in the sample of flights used for the model, as well as fewer than or equal to 80 seats.

[61] For the purposes of this report, we define large hub airports as all FAA-identified large hub airports in the United States for calendar year 2010 (the most recent year available for this list), excluding Honolulu. Federal law defines a large hub airports as those that have at least 1 percent of the passenger boardings. 49 U.S.C. § 40102(29).

[62] The specific dates we selected were Feb. 10, 2011, and Aug. 11, 2011.

[63] A logistic regression (or logit model) provides an indication of which independent variables are correlated with the dependent variable—which in this case, is a flight using a small aircraft. Moreover, it provides this measure of correlation independent of the effects of the other independent variables included in the model. It is important to note, however, that this type of statistical method only suggests correlations between variables and not causation. That is, our findings do not provide an indication that any of the independent variables we included in the model actually caused (or did not cause) an airline to use a small aircraft for a flight, but only how those variables are correlated with the use of a small aircraft.

[64] We defined Fort Lauderdale and Orlando, Florida, and Las Vegas, Nevada, as high-tourism airports.

[65] The airlines classified as "legacy" included Delta Air Lines, United Airlines, American Airlines, US Airways, and Continental Airlines. Legacy (sometimes called network) airlines support large, complex hub-and-spoke operations with thousands of employees and hundreds of aircraft (of various types), with flights to domestic communities of all sizes as well as to international destinations. The modifier "legacy" derives from the fact that these airlines were operating when the industry deregulated in 1978.

[66] Under federal statute and FAA slot control regulations applicable to Reagan National, "commuter slots" may be used only for operations with turboprop and reciprocating engine aircraft with no more than 76 seats or turbojet aircraft with fewer than 56 seats.

[67] Representatives from the remaining airline did not oppose establishing a minimum aircraft size, but did not believe that it was the best method to incent airlines to use larger aircraft.

[68] We examined airline schedule data for scheduled domestic passenger flights for Feb. 10, 2011.

[69] FAA's 80 percent minimum usage requirements pertain to how often a slot is used and not size or capacity of the aircraft using the slot.

[70] One airline representative told us that the airline would need enough slots for three transcontinental flights per day to be profitable.

[71] New York Aviation Rulemaking Committee Report, December 13, 2007.

[72] See Steven A. Morrison, "Actual, Adjacent, and Potential Competition: Estimating the Full Effects of Southwest Airlines," *Journal of Transport Economics and Policy*, Vol. 35, part 2, May 2001, and Austan Goolsbee and Chad Syverson, "How Do Incumbents Respond to the Threat of Entry? Evidence from the Major Airlines," *The Quarterly Journal of Economics* (2008).

[73] Under FAA's slot control orders for JFK, LaGuardia, and Newark, slots may not be bought or sold but may be leased or traded through the effective date of the orders, or relinquished to FAA. Under FAA slot regulations for Reagan National, slots may be bought, sold, leased, or traded, with the exception of slot exemptions, which may not be bought, sold, leased, or otherwise transferred, except through an air carrier merger or acquisition. 49 U.S.C. 41714(j).

[74] Airlines partner with other airlines on some routes and not others. Under current slot control rules, airlines are not required to provide FAA copies of slot leases (or any information regarding consideration for slots transferred). FAA slot control orders for JFK, LaGuardia,

and Newark require airlines to submit notice of a slot trade or lease to FAA in writing. Such trades or leases are subject to the confirmation and approval of FAA. The FAA slot-control regulations for Reagan National provide, in part, that requests for FAA confirmation of transfers, including leases, shall include the names of the transferor and recipient; whether the slot is to be used for an arrival or departure; the date the slot was acquired by the transferor; whether the slot has been used by the transferor for international or essential air service operations; and whether the slot will be used by the recipient for international or essential air operations, among other things. A recipient may not use a transferred slot without written confirmation from FAA.

[75] Under 49 U.S.C .§ 41712, DOT may investigate whether airlines have engaged in "unfair and deceptive practices and unfair methods of competition."

End Notes for Appendix I

[1] To obtain views from airlines on these issues, we contacted 12 airlines that serve Reagan National, had applied for beyond-perimeter slot exemptions there, or had expressed interest to FAA in serving that airport. Representatives from 11 of the 12 airlines agreed to talk with us.

[2] For the purposes of this review, we defined large hub airports as all FAA-identified large hub airports in the United States for calendar year 2010 (the most recent year available for this list), excluding Honolulu. Federal law defines large hub airports as those commercial service airports that have at least 1 percent of the passenger boardings. 49 U.S.C. § 40102(29). The large hub airports included in our study are: Hartsfield-Jackson Atlanta International, Boston Logan International, Baltimore-Washington International Thurgood Marshall, Charlotte/Douglas International, Ronald Reagan Washington National, Denver International, Dallas-Fort Worth International, Detroit Metro Wayne County, Newark Liberty International, Fort Lauderdale-Hollywood International, Dulles International, George Bush Intercontinental, John F. Kennedy International, Las Vegas McCarran International, Los Angeles International, LaGuardia International, Orlando International, Chicago Midway, Miami International, Minneapolis-St. Paul International, Chicago O'Hare International, Philadelphia International, Phoenix Sky Harbor International, San Diego International, Seattle-Tacoma International, San Francisco International, Salt Lake City International, and Tampa International.

[3] From the total slot allocations numbers, FAA removed all UPS and FedEx cargo operations from the totals. Additionally, FAA only provided slot totals for those assigned during slot-controlled hours. At JFK and Newark, slot-controlled hours are 6:00 a.m. to 10:59 p.m. Eastern Time. At LaGuardia, slot-controlled hours are 6:00 a.m. to 9:59 p.m. Eastern Time, Monday through Friday, and 12:00 p.m.to 9:59 p.m. Eastern Time on Sunday. At Reagan National, the airport is slot-controlled 24 hours a day, but we examined high-demand hours, which are from 7:00 a.m. to 9:59 p.m. Eastern Time.

[4] The specific dates we selected were Feb.10, 2011, and Aug. 11, 2011.

[5] We defined Fort Lauderdale and Orlando, Florida, and Las Vegas, Nevada, as high-tourism airports.

[6] The airlines classified as legacy included Delta Air Lines, United Airlines, American Airlines, US Airways, and Continental Airlines. Legacy (sometimes called network) airlines support large, complex hub-and-spoke operations with thousands of employees and hundreds of

aircraft (of various types), with flights to domestic communities of all sizes as well as to international destinations. The modifier "legacy" derives from the fact that these airlines were operating when the industry deregulated in 1978.

End Notes for Appendix III

[1] Slot controls at Chicago O'Hare Airport expired in 2002. In 1998, Washington National Airport was renamed Ronald Reagan Washington National Airport.

[2] 3 3 Fed. Reg. 17896 (Dec. 3, 1968).

[3] 35 Fed. Reg. 16591 (Oct. 24, 1970).

[4] 73 Fed. Reg. 29550 (May 21, 2008).

[5] Pub. L. No. 95-504, 92 Stat. 1705 (1978).

[6] 50 Fed. Reg. 52180 (Dec. 20, 1985). The 1986 allocation and withdrawal rules at the High Density Traffic Airports rules did not apply to Newark because the High Density Rule was not then in effect at that airport.

[7] GAO, *Airline Competition: Industry Operating and Marketing Practices Limit Market Entry,* GAO/RCED-90-147 (Washington, D.C.: Aug. 29, 1990).

[8] National Research Council Transportation Research Board, *Entry and Competition in the U.S. Airline Industry: Issues and Opportunities,* Special Report 255 (Washington, D.C.: 1999).

[9] Department of Transportation, *Study of the High Density Rule: Report to Congress* (Washington, D.C.: May 1995).

[10] See, e.g., H. R. Rep. No. 106-67, at 77 (1999).

[11] Wendell H. Ford Aviation Investment and Reform Act for the 21st Century (AIR-21), Pub. L. No. 106- 181, 114 Stat. 61, 108-109 (Apr. 5, 2000). AIR-21 also required the phase-out of the application of the High Density Rule at O'Hare by July 1, 2002.

[12] 66 Fed. Reg. 48157 (2001).

[13] 71 Fed. Reg. 51360 (Aug. 29, 2006).

[14] 71 Fed. Reg. 77854 (Dec. 27, 2006).

[15] Committee members included officials from DOT's Office of the Secretary and FAA, the Port Authority of New York and New Jersey, and the State of New York as well as representatives from airlines and consumer groups.

[16] 73 Fed. Reg. 3510 (Jan. 18, 2008).

[17] 7 3 Fed. Reg. 29550 (May 21, 2008).

[18] 73 Fed. Reg. 3510 (Jan. 18, 2008); 73 Fed. Reg. 29550 (May 21, 2008).

[19] 74 Fed. Reg. 845 (Jan. 8, 2009); 74 Fed. Reg. 51648 (Oct. 7, 2009); 74 Fed. Reg. 51650 (Oct. 7, 2009); 74 Fed. Reg. 51653 (Oct. 7, 2009); 76 Fed. Reg. 18616 (Apr. 4, 2011); 76 Fed. Reg. 18618 (Apr. 4, 2011); and 76 Fed. Reg. 18620 (Apr. 4, 2011).

[20] 73 Fed. Reg. 20846 (Apr. 17, 2008).

[21] 73 Fed. Reg. 29626 (May 21, 2008).

[22] 73 Fed. Reg. 60544, 60574 (Oct. 19, 2008). 73 Fed. Reg. 60544 (Oct. 10, 2008).

[23] 74 Fed. Reg. 52132 (Oct. 9, 2009); 74 Fed. Reg. 52134 (Oct. 9, 2009).

[24] See, Dec. 8, 2008 Order, Port Authority of N.Y. & N.J. v. FAA, No. 08-1329.

[25] In addition, in a legal opinion issued to multiple congressional requesters, we concluded that FAA lacked the authority to auction slots and therefore also lacked authority to retain and use auction proceeds. GAO Legal Opinion on *Federal Aviation Administration— Authority to Auction Airport Arrival and Departure Slots and to Retain and Use Auction Proceeds*, B-

316796 (Sept. 30, 2008). The United States Department of Justice, Office of Legal Counsel, opined that FAA "would not violate the [Anti-Deficiency Act] by issuing and implementing the slot auction regulation." U.S. Dep't of Justice, Office of Legal Counsel, Whether the Federal Aviation Administration's Finalizing and Implementing of Slot Auction Regulation Would Violate the Anti-Deficiency Act (Oct. 7, 2008).

[26] Omnibus Appropriations Act, 2009, Pub. L. No. 111-8, 123 Stat. 524, 921 (2009)

[27] 74 Fed. Reg. 52132 (Oct. 9, 2009); 74 Fed. Reg. 52134 (Oct. 9, 2009).

[28] See Oct. 14, 2009 Order, Port Authority of N.Y. & N.J. v. FAA, No 08-1329.

[29] Reagan National is not included in this rulemaking because it is covered under FAA's High Density Rule regulations.

[30] 75 Fed. Reg. 26322 (May 11, 2010).

[31] 76 Fed. Reg. 63702 (Oct. 13, 2011).

[32] Pub. L. No. 99-500, 100 Stat. 1783, 1783-375 (1986); Pub. L. No. 99-591, 100 Stat. 3341, 3341-376 (1986).

[33] Pub. L. No. 106-181, 114 Stat. 61 (2000).

[34] Pub. L. No. 108-176, 117 Stat. 2490 (2003).

[35] In addition, these two laws together mandated that the slot exemptions at Reagan National (1) could not be used for operations between the hours of 10:00 p.m. and 7:00 a.m. and (2) could not increase the number of operations in any 1-hour period during the hours between 7:00 a.m. and 9:59 p.m. by more than 3 operations.

[36] More specifically, these two laws together required the Secretary of Transportation to grant 24 beyond perimeter exemptions and 20 slot exemptions within the 1,250-mile perimeter.

[37] Pub. L. No. 112-95, 126 Stat. 11 (2012). In addition the FAA Modernization and Reform Act of 2012 amended the hourly limitations provision whereby such slot exemptions may not increase the number of operations in any 1-hour period during the hours between 7:00 a.m. and 9:59 p.m. by more than 5 operations

[38] Four airlines each qualified to convert one slot pair.

End Notes for Appendix V

[1] We included all large hub airports in the United States identified by FAA for calendar year 2010 (the most recent year available for this list), excluding Honolulu International.

[2] One hundred seats is generally the maximum seat capacity of most regional jet aircraft. See below for a discussion of alterative cutoffs for the definition of a small aircraft.

[3] The large hub airports included in our analysis are: Atlanta Hartsfield International, Boston Logan International, Baltimore-Washington International, Charlotte/Douglas International, Reagan National, Denver International, Dallas-Fort Worth International, Detroit Metro Wayne County, Newark, Fort Lauderdale-Hollywood International, Washington Dulles International, George Bush Intercontinental, JFK, Las Vegas McCarran International, Los Angeles International, LaGuardia, Orlando International, Chicago Midway, Miami International, Minneapolis-St. Paul International, Chicago O'Hare International, Philadelphia International, Phoenix Sky Harbor International, San Diego International Lindbergh, Seattle-Tacoma International, San Francisco International, Salt Lake City International, and Tampa International.

[4] In addition to the independent variables listed here, we tested whether scheduled flights in February (winter) had any greater likelihood of using a small aircraft than scheduled flights

in August (summer). We did not find any significant difference, so we did not include this variable in our analysis.

[5] Flight frequency also serves as a proxy for an airport hub variable that would consider whether the airport serves as a network hub for an airline.

[6] Odds are a ratio of the probability that an event will occur versus the probability that the event will not occur, or *probability / (1-probability)*. Odds ratios, therefore, are simply a ratio of odds; in general they refer to the ratio of the odds of an event (small aircraft) occurring in the exposed group (slot-controlled airports) versus the unexposed group (other large hubs).

In: Slot-Controlled Airports
Editor: Owen M. Whitaker
ISBN: 978-1-62948-350-4

Chapter 2

REAGAN NATIONAL AIRPORT: UPDATE ON CAPACITY TO HANDLE ADDITIONAL FLIGHTS AND IMPACT ON OTHER AREA AIRPORTS*

United States Government Accountability Office

ABBREVIATION

AIR-21	Wendell H. Ford Aviation Investment and Reform Act for the 21st Century
BWI	Baltimore-Washington Thurgood Marshall International Airport
DOT	Department of Transportation
DHS	Department of Homeland Security
FAA	Federal Aviation Administration
Vision 100	Vision 100 - Century of Aviation Reauthorization Act
IFR	Instrument Flight Rules
VFR	Visual Flight Rules
GAO	Government Accountability Office

* This is an edited, reformatted and augmented version of The United States Government Accountability Office publication, Report to Congressional Requesters GAO-07-352, dated February 2007.

WHY GAO DID THIS STUDY

In 1999, GAO reported that Reagan National Airport could accommodate at least 36 more slots, which are authorizations from DOT for a takeoff or landing. In 2000 and 2003, two federal statutes, known as AIR-21 and Vision 100, permitted DOT to award 44 new slots to airlines, 24 of which could be used for flights to cities more than 1,250 miles, which was the statutorily mandated limit for non stop flights from Reagan National. The DOT awards went to airlines serving six cities (Denver, Las Vegas, Los Angeles, Phoenix, Salt Lake City, and Seattle). For this year's reauthorization of the FAA, GAO was asked for an update on the capacity of Reagan National to accommodate additional slots and the effect of relaxing the perimeter rule. GAO updated its 1999 study to answer these key questions: (1) To what extent can Reagan National accommodate additional flights? (2) Since AIR-21 and Vision 100, what changes have occurred in market share and fares for flights operating between the six beyond-perimeter cities and the three Washington, D.C., area airports? In commenting on this report, DOT and the airports authority generally agree with our findings but with one exception, the airports authority disagrees with DOT's estimate of slots because it disputes their methodological assumptions. We believe the department's methodology for estimating airport capacity is appropriate.

WHAT GAO FOUND

Reagan National Airport can accommodate some additional in capacity, but airport infrastructure constrains how much can be added. FAA officials believe that some additional slots can be added, while airport officials have not made an estimate.

FAA, using the results of a 1995 DOT capacity study, determined that the airport's airside infrastructure (e.g., runways) could accommodate four additional slots per hour. Airport officials said they were unsure how many additional slots, if any, the airport could accommodate but cited several factors that could limit the airport's capacity to absorb additional slots including the limited number of gates currently available for loading airplanes and other infrastructure constraints. GAO's work shows that even if the number of slots is not increased, there is some opportunity to expand current capacity by filling unused slots and increasing the size of aircraft on existing slots to increase the number of flights and the number of passengers served. Currently, nearly 80 slots are unused because they are at early morning or late evening times and airlines have not applied to use these time slots. In addition, many of the slots reserved for large passenger jets are currently being used by smaller regional jets.

Airlines awarded slots for direct flights between Reagan National and the six beyond-perimeter cities gained significant market share in those selected cities, but the effect of these slots on competing flights operating between these cities and the other Washington, D.C. area airports is not evident. For each of the six beyond-perimeter cities, the direct flights to and from Reagan National captured the majority of passengers flying between that city and Reagan National.

In most cases, the airlines charged higher fares than competing connecting flights. GAO did not find evidence in passengers or fare data that would indicate that the new service between Reagan National and the six beyond perimeter cities had substantially affected service from Dulles or Baltimore-Washington International airports to these cities.

Cities Served with Additional Reagan National Airport Slots Permitted under AIR-21 and Vision 100, Both beyond and within 1,250 Miles

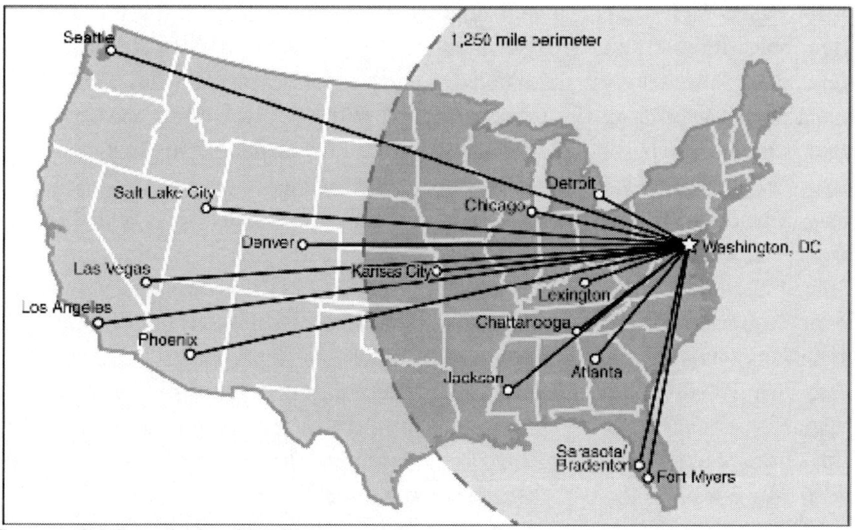

Source: GAO analysis of DOT documents.

February 28, 2007

The Honorable John Mica
Ranking Republican Member
Committee on Transportation and Infrastructure
House of Representatives

The Honorable Tom Petri
Ranking Republican Member
Subcommittee on Aviation
Committee on Transportation and Infrastructure
House of Representatives

Ronald Reagan Washington National Airport's (Reagan National) central location in the Baltimore-Washington D.C.–Northern Virginia region and proximity to the Nation's capital makes it very popular for airlines and passengers. However, since the 1960's, the federal government has restricted air traffic at Reagan National to reduce congestion and spur growth at other nearby airports. This has been achieved by controlling the number of takeoffs and landings that can occur at Reagan National each day within hourly time periods. To take off or land during any given hour at Reagan National, an airline must first obtain a slot that is an authorization from the Federal Aviation Administration (FAA) under what is called the slot rule. Each slot equates to one takeoff or landing. The airport's growth has also been constrained by limiting the distance that flights are allowed to travel. Under what is called the perimeter rule, the distance of nonstop flights that serve the airport is limited to 1,250 miles. Under this rule, passengers wishing to fly to Reagan National from airports more than 1,250 miles away must first fly to an airport within 1,250 miles and then take another flight continuing on to Reagan National. The slot rule also grants 12 slots per hour to general aviation or other aircraft that do not operate on a scheduled basis, such as corporate jets or military planes. Prior to the terrorist attacks of September 11, 2001, there were over 40,000 annual general aviation and unscheduled flights to and from Reagan National but since then, the Department of Homeland Security (DHS) restrictions on general aviation flights in the national capital region have drastically curtailed the use of these slots to about 200 over the past year.

In 1999, we analyzed legislative proposals to increase the number of slots at Reagan National and reported that the airport could accommodate at least 36 more slots per day and that adding beyond-perimeter slots would have limited effects on nearby Dulles International (Dulles) and Baltimore-Washington Thurgood Marshall International Airport (BWI).[1] The rule that governs the number of slots at Reagan National limits the number of takeoffs or landings to 48 commercial slots per hour occurs during an 18- hour period (6:00 a.m. to midnight) over the airport's 24-hour operating day.[2]

In 2000 and 2003, two federal statutes —AIR-21[3] and Vision 100[4] increased the number of slots and for the first time allowed for exemptions to be granted to the perimeter rule. The statutes granted exemptions to the existing rules, adding 44 slots per day during a 15-hour period and allowing 24 of these slots for flights of more than 1,250 miles—flights longer than 1,250 miles are called beyond-perimeter flights.[5] In effect, given the 15- hour period for these slot exemptions, this added on average three commercial slots per hour. The Department of Transportation (DOT) awarded these new slots exemptions to airlines and routes that best met specified criteria.[6] The 24 beyond-perimeter slot exemptions were awarded to airlines operating flights from six airports–Denver International (Denver), Phoenix-Sky Harbor (Phoenix), McCarran International (Las Vegas), Los Angeles International (Los Angeles), Salt Lake City International (Salt Lake City), and Seattle-Tacoma International (Seattle).

In anticipation of this year's reauthorization of FAA, you asked for an update of GAO's 1999 report on Reagan National's ability to accommodate additional capacity and the effect of relaxing the perimeter rule. To provide this update, we addressed these key questions:

- To what extent can Reagan National accommodate additional flights?
- Since AIR-21 and Vision 100, for the six beyond-perimeter airports, what changes have occurred in market share and fares at Reagan National and what changes have occurred in the number of passengers and fares at Dulles and BWI airports?

To identify the number of additional slots Reagan National can accommodate and the factors affecting existing capacity, we reviewed FAA flight data and gate utilization data obtained from the Metropolitan Washington Airports Authority (airports authority) and we interviewed DOT, FAA and airport officials. To assess the changes in passenger levels and fares at Washington area airports and the six beyond-perimeter airports, we analyzed DOT origin and destination ticket data and interviewed officials at all three Washington, D.C., area airports. We reviewed the reliability of these data and concluded that they were sufficiently reliable for our purposes. We conducted our work from July 2006 to February 2007 in accordance with generally accepted government auditing standards. More details about the scope and the methodology of our work are presented in appendix I.

RESULTS IN BRIEF

Reagan National Airport can accommodate some additional capacity, but airport infrastructure constrains how much can be added. FAA officials believe that some new slots for flights can be added. Based on DOT's 1995 capacity study, FAA estimates that the airport's airside infrastructure—principally runways—could presently accommodate four additional slots per hour or 60 daily slots based on a 15-hour operating period. Airport officials disagree with FAA's method of measuring capacity and said they were unsure how many additional slots, if any, the airport could accommodate and cited several factors as contributing to their uncertainty. For example, officials said that the airport's ability to absorb the slot exemptions granted under AIR-21 and Vision 100 has been aided by the near absence of general aviation flights. Whether general aviation will return to the previous levels is currently unknown; but in its absence, airport officials said that some runway capacity remains unutilized. Airport officials also said that if additional slots are added, the airport's ability to accommodate more aircraft will be limited by such factors as the lack of gates for loading airplanes and other infrastructure constraints. Our analysis shows that even if the number of slots is not increased, there is some opportunity for expanding capacity under current rules. Currently, 78 existing slots remain unused—mostly during the early morning and late evening hours—and airlines have not applied to use these slots. In addition, the capacity of the existing slots could also be increased by using larger planes to carry more passengers. Currently, smaller commuter aircraft, carrying a maximum of 76 passengers, are being widely used in slots designated for larger jets.

Airlines awarded slot exemptions for direct flights between Reagan National and the six beyond-perimeter airports gained a significant market share of traffic for those selected routes, but the effect of these flights on competing flights operating between these airports and the other Washington, D.C., area airports is not evident. For most of the six beyond-perimeter airports, the direct flights to and from Reagan National captured the majority of passengers flying between that airport and Reagan National. In most cases, the airlines charge higher average fares than on competing connecting flights.

For example, in the Salt Lake City market, Delta Airlines (both nonstop and connecting flights) carries nearly 60 percent of the passenger traffic serving Reagan National and charges on average nearly $50 more for a direct flight than competing airlines charge for connecting flights between Salt Lake City and Reagan National. We did not find evidence about passengers or fares at Dulles or BWI for the six beyond-perimeter airports that would indicate that the new beyond-perimeter service to Reagan National had substantially affected flights between these two airports and the six beyond-perimeter airports.

DOT and the airports authority provided comments on a draft of this report and generally agree with our findings with one exception. While the airports authority believes it can accommodate some additional capacity it disagrees with the department's estimate of how many additional slots it can accommodate because it disputes its methodological assumptions. DOT believes its methodology, which attempts to consider capacity under a variety of weather conditions, is more appropriate than the airport authority's preference to estimate capacity only under poor weather conditions. We believe the department's methodology for estimating airport capacity is more appropriate because the airport authority's approach would leave large amounts of airfield capacity unused because a significantly higher capacity could be achieved during better weather conditions. DOT and the airports authority provided overall comments and technical clarifications in some areas of this report. We have addressed these comments and clarifications where appropriate. The airport authority's comments and our responses are presented in appendix II.

BACKGROUND

Reagan National Airport was built by the federal government and opened on June 16, 1941, on the western bank of the Potomac River, across from Washington, D.C.[7] Reagan National currently has three runways and two terminals with a total of 44 gates or passenger loading ramps for use by air carriers. The airport currently handles 400 daily departures to 75 cities, offered by 20 different airlines (this includes commuter airlines, which operate solely for the major carriers). Terminal A, the original terminal, has 9 gates, and Terminal B/C, which opened in 1997, has 35 gates, 100 ticket counters, and 12 baggage claim areas. In 2005, 17.8 million passengers used Reagan National. The airline with the largest number of flights at Reagan National is US

Airways, which controls 44 percent of the commercial slots. The next largest operators are Delta Airlines and American Airlines, which have 14 percent of the commercial slots each. During 2005, these three airlines together accounted for nearly 60 percent of total passenger enplanements at the airport.

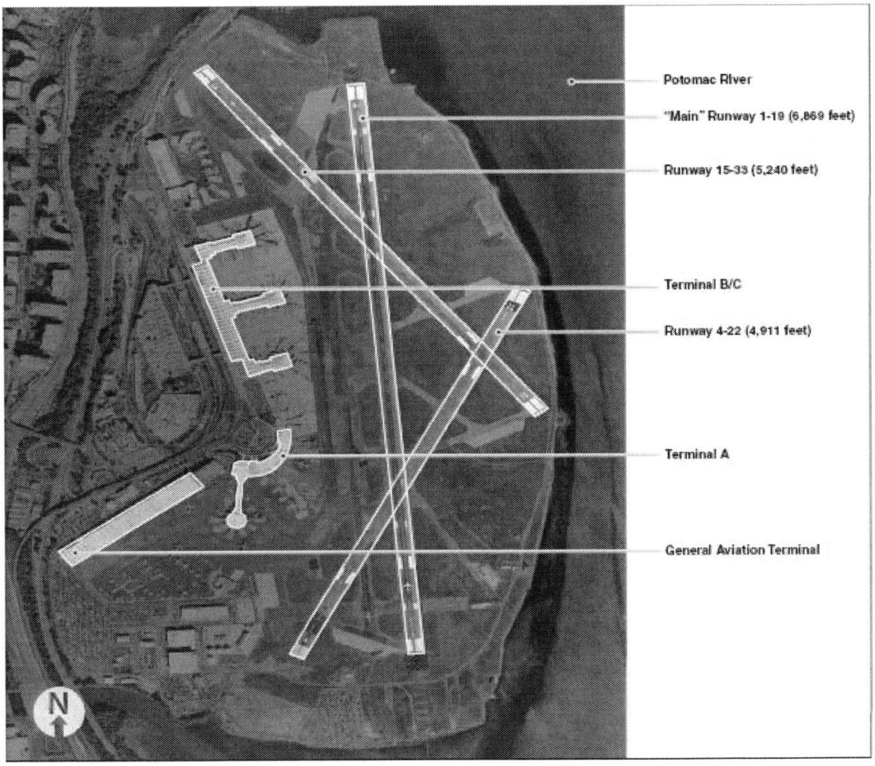

Source: FAA.

Figure 1. Layout of Reagan National Airport.

In 1969, FAA applied special air traffic rules to certain airports facing increasing delays and congestion that it designated as high-density airports: Chicago-O'Hare; New York's LaGuardia and Kennedy; Newark, New Jersey; and Reagan National (DOT dropped Newark's designation as a high-density airport in October 1970). Because of the restricted number of allowable flights, these airports are generally known as slot-controlled, and the special air traffic rules governing the allowable number of flights are referred to as slot rules, or high-density rules.

The number of hourly slots at Reagan National is controlled by the federal government. Since 1969, the federal government has restricted the number of commercial takeoffs and landings at Reagan National. Currently, the number allowed is 48 per hour: 37 for air carriers and 11 for commuter aircraft.[8] Table 1 shows the number of slots per hour by type of aircraft permitted under the slot rule. FAA authorizes general aviation or unscheduled aircraft to make an additional 12 takeoffs or landings during each hour for a total of 60 slots per hour.

Table 1. Slots Per Hour by Carrier

Type	Slots per hour
Air carrier[a]	37[b]
Commuter	11
General aviation/unscheduled	12
Total	60

Source: GAO analysis of DOT documents.

[a]Can be used by commuter but not vice versa (14 C.F.R. § 93.123).

[b]The original limit on the number of air carrier slots was 40 per hour. FAA reduced it to 37 in 1981 and increased the number of commuter slots from 8 to 11.

A perimeter rule has been in place at Reagan National since May 1966 restricting airlines from operating nonstop flights between Reagan National and airports further than a specified distance. The FAA previously had concerns that allowing long-range jets to fly into Reagan National would create a noise problem and hamper growth of the newly built Dulles International Airport. As a result, with the airlines agreeing, the Civil Aeronautics Board approved a 650-mile perimeter, with exceptions of seven cities between 650 and 1,000 miles away that enjoyed grandfather status as of December 1, 1965.

In 1986, the Congress codified the slot and perimeter rules into federal statute as part of the Metropolitan Washington Airports Act of 1986.[9] The act led to the transfer of authority over Reagan National and Dulles from the federal government to the Metropolitan Washington Airports Authority and set the perimeter at 1,250 miles, which allowed nonstop flights as far as Houston and Dallas.

Two federal statutes enacted in 2000 and 2003 modified the slot and perimeter rules at Reagan National Airport. AIR-21 and Vision 100 effectively added up to three commercial slots per hour and for the first time designated some slots for flights beyond the 1,250 mile perimeter. AIR-21 and Vision

100, combined, allowed the Secretary of Transportation to award 22 roundtrips, 12 with service to airports beyond the perimeter and 10 with service to airports within the perimeter. Figure 2 shows each market by number of slots and airline.

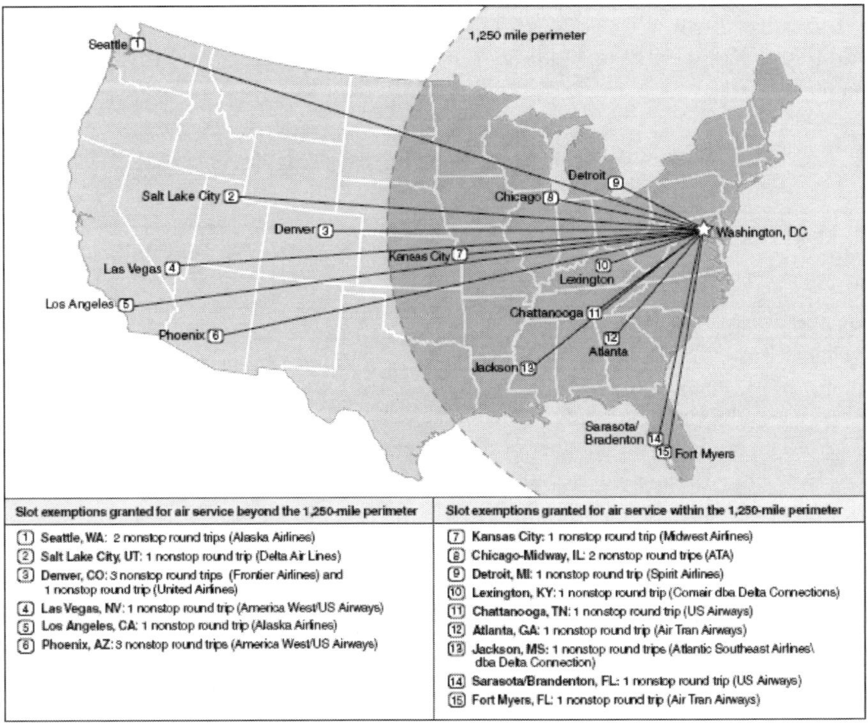

Slot exemptions granted for air service beyond the 1,250-mile perimeter	Slot exemptions granted for air service within the 1,250-mile perimeter
(1) **Seattle, WA:** 2 nonstop round trips (Alaska Airlines)	(7) **Kansas City:** 1 nonstop round trip (Midwest Airlines)
(2) **Salt Lake City, UT:** 1 nonstop round trip (Delta Air Lines)	(8) **Chicago-Midway, IL:** 2 nonstop round tripes (ATA)
(3) **Denver, CO:** 3 nonstop round trips (Frontier Airlines) and 1 nonstop round trip (United Airlines)	(9) **Detroit, MI:** 1 nonstop round trip (Spirit Airlines)
(4) **Las Vegas, NV:** 1 nonstop round trip (America West/US Airways)	(10) **Lexington, KY:** 1 nonstop round trip (Comair dba Delta Connections)
(5) **Los Angeles, CA:** 1 nonstop round trip (Alaska Airlines)	(11) **Chattanooga, TN:** 1 nonstop round trip (US Airways)
(6) **Phoenix, AZ:** 3 nonstop round tripes (America West/US Airways)	(12) **Atlanta, GA:** 1 nonstop round trip (Air Tran Airways)
	(13) **Jackson, MS:** 1 nonstop round tripes (Atlantic Southeast Airlines\ dba Delta Connection)
	(14) **Sarasota/Brandenton, FL:** 1 nonstop round trip (US Airways)
	(15) **Fort Myers, FL:** 1 nonstop round trip (Air Tran Airways)

Source: GAO analysis of DOT documents.

Figure 2. Summary of Slot Exemptions Granted by DOT under AIR-21 and Vision 100 as of September 2006.

Two other commercial airports serve the Baltimore-Washington metropolitan area—Dulles International Airport and Baltimore-Washington International Thurgood Marshall Airport (BWI). Dulles opened on November 19, 1962. The federal government built Dulles, located approximately 30 miles west of Washington, D.C., in part to provide a facility for nonstop and connecting and international air carrier traffic into the Washington, D.C. area. In 2005, Dulles handled 27 million passengers. BWI, built by the city of Baltimore and originally named Friendship International Airport, was opened on June 24, 1950. BWI, which is owned and operated by the state of

Maryland, is located 10 miles southwest of Baltimore and approximately 30 miles northeast of Washington, D.C. In 2005, BWI handled 19.7 million passengers.

FAA Indicates Some Additional Capacity Could Be Added, but Airports Authority Cites Airport Infrastructure Constraints as an Obstacle

According to FAA officials, whose estimate is based on airside capacity (principally runways) and not landside infrastructure (such as terminals and parking facilities), Reagan National can presently accommodate four additional slots per hour. Airport officials disagree on the basis for FAA's estimate and cite the unknown future course of general aviation at the airport and the limited capacity of airport infrastructure (such as gates, baggage handling areas, and parking) to handle more commercial flights. Airport officials were unsure of how many additional flights, if any, the airport could accommodate. Even without increasing the number of slots, there are opportunities to accommodate more flights and passengers. Some current slots remain unused during early morning or late evening hours, and some slots designated for air carriers are being used for smaller commuter aircraft.

FAA Estimates Airport Can Accommodate Additional Slots

According to FAA, Reagan National's overall runway capacity can presently accommodate about four additional hourly slots above the current slot allocation under the high-density rule.[10] FAA continues to rely on the DOT's study of the high-density rule that it conducted in 1995.[11] The study estimated that the airport's balanced capacity is 67 flights per hour, or 4 more than what is currently in place, resulting in an additional 60 flights per day based on an 15-hour operating period.[12] The study predated the exclusion of general aviation after September 11. The study concluded that FAA's traffic programs and procedures could safely accommodate the increase, but it also said the increase was likely to result in more delays. In 2004, the most current year for which this data are available, Reagan National experienced an average delay time of 5 minutes, one of the lowest in the nation for large hub commercial airports.[13]

Airports Authority Questions Reagan National's Capacity to Accommodate Additional Slots

Airport officials disagree with FAA's estimate because it assumes balanced capacity, whereas the airport prefers to measure capacity differently. Airport officials stated any measurement of capacity should be based on poor weather conditions and Instrument Flight Rules (IFR).[14] FAA and GAO believe balanced capacity is a more appropriate method for determining an airport's capacity than the method suggested by the airports authority. The 1995 DOT study points out that estimating capacity under IFR conditions, when the airfield is at the lowest level of available capacity does not ensure steady airfield availability. In practice, this approach would leave large amounts of airfield capacity unused because a significantly higher capacity could be achieved during the better weather conditions under which Visual Flight Rules (VFR) apply.[15] According to data from DOT, less than 1 percent of air traffic operations at Reagan National from November 2005 to November 2006 were delayed because of weather conditions.

Assuming capacity under IFR conditions, airport officials raised two issues that would limit growth at the airport. The first issue is the potential return of general aviation flights. Airport official said the absence of general aviation flights helped the airport to absorb the additional slots that were authorized under AIR-21 and Vision 100. After September 2001, DHS banned general aviation flights around the national capital region.[16] Prior to the September 11 terrorist attacks, the airport handled 40,000 to 50,000 unscheduled aircraft flights including general aviation, annually.

Since October 2005, general aviation flights have been allowed to return, but only under very restrictive conditions, resulting in very little activity at Reagan National.[17] According to airport officials, between October 2005 and August 2006, for example, the airport had fewer than 200 general aviation flights. Figure 3 shows the level of flights of all types of aircraft since January 2001. As the figure shows, traffic for all types dropped after September 11, 2001, but commercial traffic (commuter and air carrier) has basically returned to pre-September 11 levels. By contrast, general aviation has not done so.

According to airport officials, as a result of the significantly diminished presence of general aviation, some airside capacity remains, but commercial aviation might not be able to use it all. A key reason is that commercial aircraft require the longer main runway for takeoff and landings, while many general aviation aircraft can use the shorter runways for takeoff and landing.

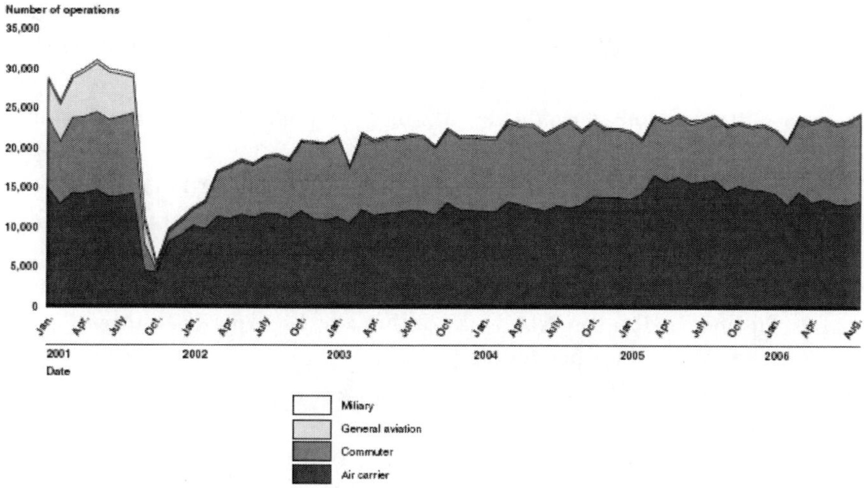

Source: GAO analysis of FAA tower data.

Figure 3. Number of Flights at Reagan National By Aircraft, January 2001- August 2006.

The second issue airport officials raised as limiting capacity is infrastructure limitations. These limitations involve several aspects of the airport's infrastructure.

- *Passenger Loading Gates.* According to airport officials, the number of gates affects the ability to add more slots. Every gate at the airport is currently leased to airlines with flights at the airport, known as tenant airlines. Airlines wishing to begin flights at the airport, known as new entrants, can make arrangements with tenant airlines to share a gate, but a tenant airline is not required to share its gate if its schedule does not allow it.[18] A recent analysis by the airport shows that some gates are available during certain parts of the day. For example, during October 2006, some gates were unused during both peak and nonpeak times, primarily those in the older and less desirable terminal A. During the 18-hour operating period, gates in terminal A were unused 46 percent of the time, while gates in terminal B/C were unused 22 percent of the time. Most of the available time periods are during nonpeak hours.
- *Terminal Facilities.* Officials said Reagan National has limited capacity to expand terminal facilities such as ticket counters and

baggage handling areas due to the lack of space on the airport property. If additional slots are permitted, existing tenant airlines might be able to use their existing facilities more fully, but new entrant airlines may have difficulty obtaining the necessary terminal facilities, especially at peak periods during the day. For the recent slots awarded under AIR-21 and Vision 100, the airports authority has been able to accommodate new entrants with gates and other facilities. However, airport officials said that such accommodation has become increasingly difficult. Officials from Alaska Airlines, one of the newer airlines at Reagan National, told us that its experience in getting the needed facilities has been positive.

- *Parking Facilities.* According to airport officials, limited parking at the airport could make it difficult to accommodate additional passengers, resulting from increased slots. Passengers have a variety of ways to access the airport terminal, including rail transit, taxis, shuttle services, and private car. For those who drive their own cars, the airport provides over 7,900 parking spaces. According to airport officials, the parking facility is running at or near capacity with the existing flight schedule. For example, over a 12-month period from November 2005 to October 2006, two of the four parking garages reached capacity 100 days or more. In order to help mitigate some of this pressure, the airport plans to add an additional deck to the current parking structure. This additional parking deck would provide 850 more spaces and is slated for completion in 2010.

Opportunities Exist to Expand Current Capacity at Reagan National

In two ways, Reagan National's current capacity under the existing slot limits could be expanded. First, the airport has available slots during certain parts of the day, though they are for less desirable times. Of the total 912 daily slots available for airlines, 834 are currently allocated and approximately 78 slots are unused.[19] Each of these unused slots falls either in the early morning (between 6:00 and 7:00) or in the late evening (between 9:00 and midnight), which suggests that no existing airlines and most likely no new entrants wish to initiate new service with a schedule limited to these hours.[20] According to airport officials, these slots remain unallocated because there is less demand for passenger service during these hours and because noise restrictions after 10 p.m. require quieter aircraft.[21] The second way in which current capacity could be expanded is to reduce the number of smaller commuter planes using slots that are allocated for larger jet planes that carry more passengers. For example, FAA data show that in August 2006, commuter flights used nearly double the slots that were designated for commuter flights (see table 2). For example, on one route, between Raleigh-Durham and Reagan National, DOT data show that in November 2006, two carriers operated an average of 26 daily flights using commuter jets, which have a maximum capacity of 76 seats, although larger jets were designated for the slots used for the commuter flights. FAA and airport officials acknowledged that commuter aircraft often use air carrier slots, but noted that this practice is permissible under federal regulation.

Table 2. Reagan National Slots Allocated and Used by Aircraft Type, August 2006

Type	Total monthly number of slots	Actual flights	Percentage of slots utilized
Air carrier	22,320[a]	13,333	60%
Commuter	6,138	10,681	174%[b]

Source: GAO analysis of FAA tower data.

[a] includes slot exemptions added under AIR-21 and Vision 100.

[b] Commuter reflects both commuter slots and air carrier slots used by commuters.

Airlines awarded slots for nonstop service between Reagan National and airports beyond the 1,250 mile perimeter have been able to gain a significant market share of traffic for routes. The price they charge for this direct service is generally higher than the price for flights requiring a connection. We did not find evidence that Dulles or BWI traffic or fares were affected by the beyond perimeter flights to Reagan National.

Airlines with Nonstop Service between Beyond-Perimeter Airports and Reagan National Gained Significant Market Share of Traffic in Those Markets, While the Effect on Flights to Other Area Airports Is Not Evident

For each of the six beyond-perimeter airports, the airlines awarded slots for nonstop service between Reagan National and those airports gained significant market share of passenger traffic over a short period of time. For example, in the Denver market, Frontier Airlines, had no nonstop passenger traffic between Denver and Reagan National before it was awarded two slots (one daily roundtrip) in August 2000 and four additional slots (two more daily roundtrips) in 2004, and it now has garnered nearly 60 percent of the passenger traffic to Reagan National from Denver (see table 3). United Airlines, which was awarded two slots (one daily roundtrip) in the same market in 2004, now has 15 percent of the market. Between Frontier and United Airlines, the two carriers' nonstop routes have nearly three-fourths of the Denver-Reagan National traffic.

Table 3. Share of Passenger Traffic by Airline

Market	Airline	Year slot award service initiated	Before slot award average market sharea	Current average market share (1st qtr 2006)
Denver	Frontier	2000	0%	59%
	United	2004	0.5%	15%
Los Angeles	Alaska	2004	0%	43%
Las Vegas	America West	2000	0%	23%
Phoenix	America West	2000	12%	61%
Salt Lake City	Delta	2003	0%	59%
Seattle	Alaska	2001	0%	62%

Source: GAO analysis of DOT's origin and destination survey.

[a] Average market share data based on the year before award.

Table 4. Average One-way Fares for Nonstop and Connecting Flights to Reagan National in Beyond-Perimeter Airports (2005)

Market	Airline	Nonstop flight	Connecting flight
Denver	Frontier	$159	n/a
	United	$237	$151
Los Angeles	Alaska	$178	$190
Las Vegas	America West	$180	$176
Phoenix	America West	$251	$176
Salt Lake City	Delta	$250	$201
Seattle	Alaska	$247	$226

Source: GAO analysis of DOT's origin and destination survey.

Airlines with beyond-perimeter slots generally charge higher fares than are charged for connecting flights to and from Reagan National (see table 4).

In half of the cases the nonstop fare was on average $25 to $50 higher than the connecting flight fares to and from Reagan National. Los Angeles is the only market in which the average direct fare is less than the average fare for flights with connections.

The Effect of Beyond-Perimeter Slots on Area Airports Is Not Evident

We did not find evidence that beyond-perimeter flights to and from Reagan National affected flights from the same airports to or from Dulles or BWI. We analyzed fare and passenger data for flights between Dulles and BWI and those airports and for all traffic serving Dulles and BWI. In doing so, we observed that the data did not produce any distinguishable trends or patterns that would indicate that beyond-perimeter slots at Reagan had any effect on fares or passenger levels at either Dulles or BWI.

Overall, Dulles has experienced growth in traffic and a decline in fares, while BWI has experienced little overall change in traffic or fares from 1999 to 2005.

To assess whether the introduction of new nonstop beyond-perimeter routes into Reagan National affected service between the same six airports and Dulles or BWI, we compared the percentage change in average fares and total passengers, from 1999 through 2005 for travel between each of the six beyond-perimeter airports and Dulles and BWI against the overall percentage change in annual average fares and passengers for all traffic serving Dulles and BWI.

As the figures below illustrate, some routes experienced greater or lesser changes relative to overall changes at the airport, but no consistent trends were apparent.

- Dulles annual airport passenger traffic grew from 1999 to 2005, from 19.7 million to 27 million, a 37 percent increase. We did not find any patterns or trends that would suggest that the changes to the perimeter rule at Reagan National had affected fares or service between Dulles and these six airports. (See figs. 4 and 5). Airports authority officials stated they had no reason to believe that these limited beyond-perimeter awards affected Dulles. Rather, the officials noted, the airport's fares and passenger traffic were significantly affected by its experience with low-fare carrier, Independence Air, which had a large growth of flights at Dulles but has now gone out of business.

For overall passenger traffic between Dulles and the six airports, as figure 4 shows, we did not find evidence that the beyond-perimeter slots at Reagan National affected passenger levels.

For example, passenger traffic between Dulles and some airports grew faster than overall airport traffic despite the introduction of nonstop flights to Reagan National.

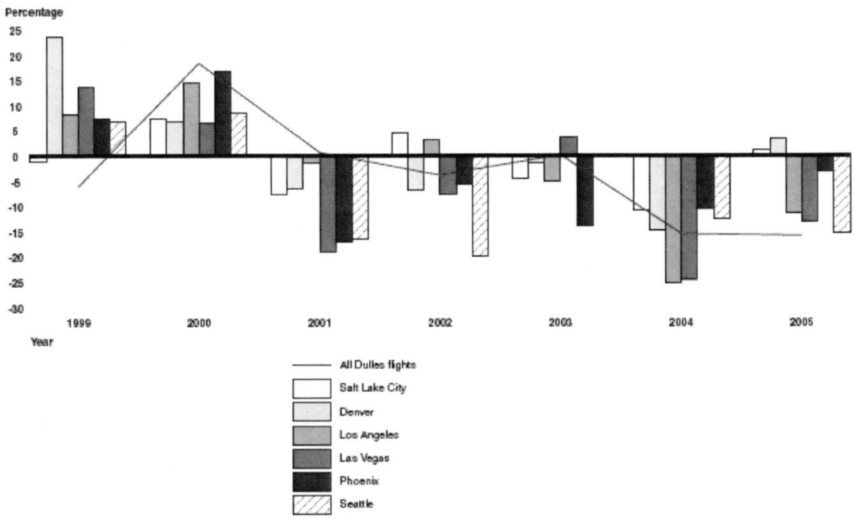

Source: GAO analysis of DOT's origin and destination survey.

Figure 4. Annual Percentage Change in Passengers for All Dulles Flights and Flights between Dulles and Six Beyond-Perimeter Airports, 1999-2005.

- BWI airport passenger traffic grew from 17.4 million in 1999 to 19.7 million in 2005. But, similar to Dulles, we found no patterns or trends in passengers or fares between BWI and the six airports that would suggest that changes to the beyond-perimeter rule at Reagan National had an impact on flights at BWI. (See figs. 6 and 7). Officials from BWI stated that changes to the slot and perimeter rule did not adversely affect BWI and noted other factors, notably US Airways reduction of its commuter service at BWI.

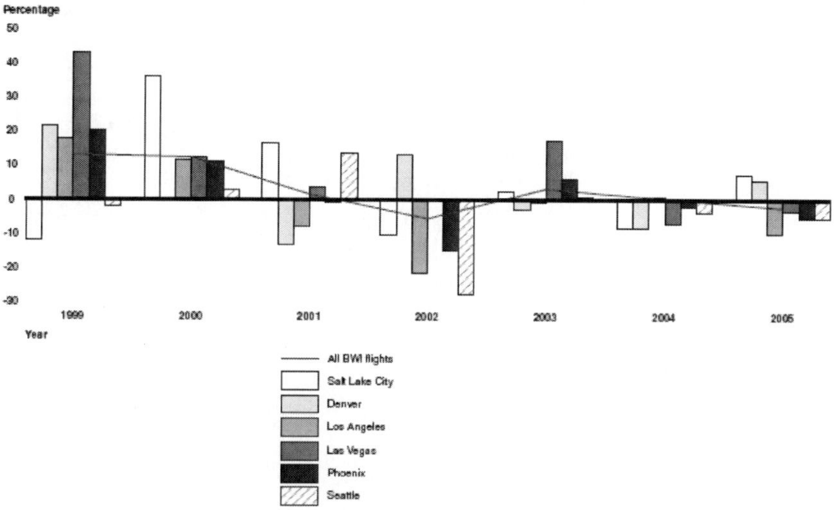

Source: GAO analysis of DOT's origin and destination survey.

Figure 5. Annual Percentage Change in Average Fares for All Dulles Flights and Flights between Dulles and Six Beyond-Perimeter Airports, 1999-2005.

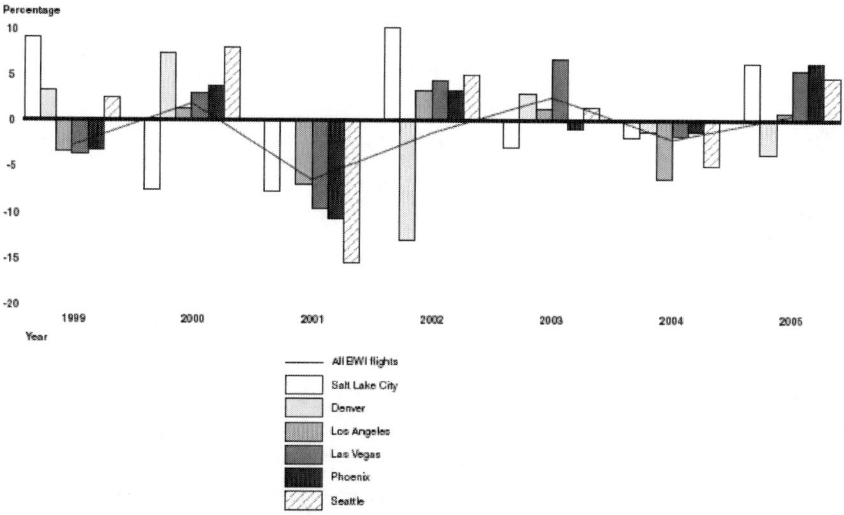

Source: GAO analysis of DOT's origin and destination survey.

Figure 6. Annual Percentage Change in Passengers for All BWI Flights and Flights between BWI and Six Beyond-Perimeter Airports, 1999-2005.

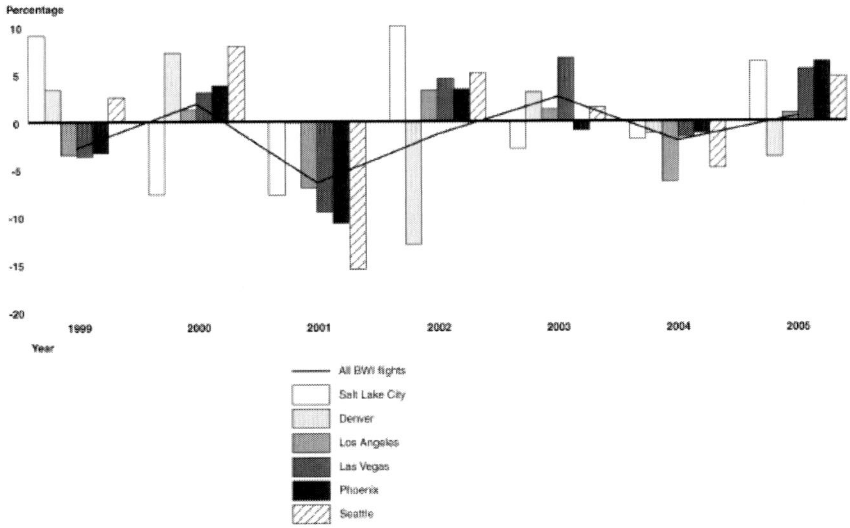

Source: GAO analysis of DOT's origin and destination survey.

Figure 7. Annual Percentage Change in Average Fares for All BWI Flights and Flights between BWI and Six Beyond-Perimeter Airports, 1999-2005.

AGENCY COMMENTS

We provided copies of this report to DOT and the airports authority. We received comments from the Office of the Deputy Assistant Secretary for Aviation and International Affairs, Department of Transportation. DOT acknowledges that all available slots at Reagan National Airport are not used to maximum effect and agreed that there are a number of reasons for this, including curfew restrictions, the commercial viability of slots in the early morning or late evening under current regulations, and the concentration of the majority of slot holdings among a relatively small number of carriers. DOT also recognizes that the underutilization of slots is exacerbated by the fact that carriers can use commuter aircraft in slots designated for large aircraft but are legally prohibited from using large aircraft in slots designated for commuter aircraft. In addition, other statutory restrictions, such as the perimeter rule, contribute to the underutilization of slots and prevent market forces from producing the maximum public benefit from these scarce assets. For example, the early departure and late arrival times at other airports are often used by airlines to operate overnight "red eye" or other long-haul flights. Regulations governing operations at Reagan National, such as the perimeter rule, prevent carriers from using such scheduling and fleet assignment techniques to maximize the value of slots and facilities at that airport. While we do not disagree with DOT's observations, we also recognize that any changes in the commuter slot or perimeter rules at Reagan National would have competitive implications for airlines and the communities they serve. Assessing these effects was beyond the scope of our study. Finally, DOT offered technical comments, which we have incorporated as appropriate.

The airports authority commented that with one exception the report accurately reflects the situation at Reagan National. While the airports authority believes that the airport can accommodate some additional capacity, it is something less than the 4 slots per hour as suggested by DOT. The airports authority still disagrees with the basis for DOT's 1995 estimate of 67 slots per hour under the High-Density Rule, just as it did in response to our 1999 report on this matter. The airports authority believes that maximum capacity should be based on IFR conditions, that is, capacity under adverse weather conditions. Instead, DOT bases its estimate of maximum capacity on a mix of IFR and VFR traffic, a methodology that we endorsed in 1999 and still do today. We believe, as does DOT, that balanced capacity is a superior method for determining the airport's capacity because it accounts for the operation of aircraft during all weather conditions. The airports authority offered technical comments, which we have incorporated as appropriate.

Gerald L. Dillingham, Ph.D.
Director,
Physical Infrastructure Issues

APPENDIX I: SCOPE AND METHODOLOGY

To determine how many additional slots Reagan National Airport can accommodate, we analyzed Federal Aviation Administration (FAA) and Metropolitan Washington Airports Authority (airports authority) operational data, reviewed prior capacity studies, and interviewed airports authority, FAA, and Department of Transportation (DOT) officials. This analysis included reviewing data on the number and type of aircraft using the slots and how this usage was dispersed during the day and by which runway. We also reviewed the data contained in the 1995 study done by the DOT on the high-density rule and reviewed the basis for DOT's capacity estimates. In addition, we analyzed airports authority gate utilization data and airline leases to determine the extent to which gate space at the airport is unused. Finally, we interviewed officials from the DOT, FAA, airports authority and other stakeholders about Reagan National's current and future capacity.

To assess traffic between Washington, D.C., area airports and the six beyond-perimeter airports for which nonstop service to Reagan National was awarded since 1999, we analyzed DOT's Origin and Destination ticket data; we used these data to examine changes in fares and passenger levels between Reagan National, Dulles International (Dulles) and Baltimore-Washington Thurgood Marshall International Airport (BWI), and these airports. We also interviewed airports authority and BWI officials. For this analysis, we conducted a historical look at traffic between the six airports and the three Washington-Baltimore area airports. We obtained the ticket data from BACK Aviation Solutions, a private contractor that provides these data to interested parties. We used these data to examine trends in passenger and fares to identify any changes in traffic and fares between the six beyond-perimeter airports and Reagan National, Dulles and BWI airports. To assess the reliability of these data, we reviewed the quality control procedures applied to these data, and subsequently determined that the data were sufficiently reliable for our purposes. We conducted our review from July 2006 through February 2007 in accordance with generally accepted government auditing standards.

End Notes

[1] GAO/RCED- 99-234.

[2] 14 C.F.R. § 93, Subpart K.

[3] The Wendell H. Ford Aviation Investment and Reform Act for the 21st Century (AIR-21) Pub. L. No. 106-81 (Apr. 5, 2000).

[4] The Century of Aviation Reauthorization Act (Vision 100) Pub. L. No. 108-176 (Dec. 13, 2003).

[5] AIR-21 and Vision 100 permitted slots to operate during 7:00 a.m through 9:59 p.m.

[6] Congress set forth slot exemption criteria, and DOT granted exemptions to airlines whose service would (for beyond-perimeter exemptions) (1) provide air transportation with domestic network benefits beyond the 1,250-mile perimeter, (2) increase competition by new entrant air carriers or in multiple markets, (3) not reduce travel options for communities served by small hub airports and medium hub airports within the 1,250-mile perimeter and, (4) not result in meaningfully increased travel delays. For within-perimeter slot exemptions, DOT distributed exemptions in a manner that promoted air transportation: (1) by new entrant air carriers and limited incumbent air carriers, (2) to communities without existing nonstop air transportation to Reagan National, (3) to small communities,

(4) that will provide competitive nonstop air transportation on a nonstop route to Reagan National, or (5) that will produce the maximum competitive benefits, including low fares.

[7] The airport's official name changed from Washington National to Ronald Reagan Washington National Airport under Pub. L. No. 105-154, 112 Stat 3 (1998).

[8] Commuter aircraft are generally turboprop or small jet aircraft seating 76 or fewer passengers. Within the past few years, several commuter airlines have begun using small jet aircraft (regional jets) in their fleets. To avoid confusion throughout the remainder of this report, we will refer to all commuter aircraft, regardless of whether they are regional jets or turboprops, as commuter aircraft.

[9] Pub. L. No. 99-500, 100 Stat. 1783-375, Pub. L. No. 99-591, 100 Stat. 3341-378.

[10] The slot exemptions permitted by AIR-21 and Vision 100 used three of the seven additional slots DOT originally estimated in 1995.

[11] U.S. DOT, Report to the Congress: A Study of the High Density Rule, May 1995.

[12] "Balanced capacity" refers to the average ability of an airport's runways to support a certain number of operations per hour under varying weather and wind conditions.

[13] A large hub enplanes (number of passengers boarded) at least 1 percent of all passengers.

[14] IFR governs procedures for conducting aircraft operations during weather conditions when the cloud ceiling is less than 1,000 feet and/or visibility is less than 3 miles, requiring certain aircraft separations and other operating standards.

[15] VFR governs procedures for conducting aircraft operations when the cloud ceiling is more than 1,000 feet and visibility is 3 miles or more. Airport capacity under these conditions is generally significantly higher than conditions under IFR.

[16] Special flight restrictions in the National Capital Region, where Reagan National is located, have been in place since September 2001, primarily affecting general aviation.

[17] According to FAA, airports authority, and the general aviation community, activity is low due to the DHS security requirements. National Business Aviation Association officials told us that the restrictions are onerous and force general aviation users to other area general aviation airports. As part of this reintroduction plan, DHS is required to conduct 1-year review of the first phase of the security program. To date, DHS has not conducted this review. We also asked if DHS had any time frame for further easing of the restrictions, but DHS did not have a date.

[18] Under DOT grant requirements, airports unable to accommodate an airline's request for access to gates or other facilities shall submit a report to DOT outlining the nature of the request, why the request could not be accommodated, and a time frame when, if any, the airport will be able to accommodate the request.

[19] Includes slot exemptions granted under AIR-21 and Vision 100.

[20] FAA controls the allocation of available air carrier and commuter slots at Reagan National during an 18-hour period every day, from 6:00 am until midnight.

[21] Between 10 p.m. and 7 a.m. air carriers are required to meet the airports authority's noise regulation.

INDEX

D

E

F

G

H

I

L

M

N

O

P

Q

R

S

T

U

V

W

Y